PLAY OF DOUBLE SENSES

SPENSER'S
FAERIE QUEENE

PLAY OF DOUBLE SENSES

SPENSER'S
FAERIE QUEENE

A. BARTLETT GIAMATTI

W.W. NORTON & COMPANY

New York • London

First published as a Norton paperback 1990

Library of Congress Cataloging in Publication Data

Giamatti, A. Bartlett.
  Play of double senses: Spenser's Faerie queene.
  (Prentice-Hall Landmarks in literature series)
  Bibliography: p.
  1. Spenser, Edmund, 1552?–1599. Faerie queene.
I. Title.
PR2358.A3G5   821'.3   74-18253

ISBN 0-393-30631-3

W.W. Norton & Company, Inc.
500 Fifth Avenue, New York, N.Y. 10110
W.W. Norton & Company Ltd.
37 Great Russell Street, London WC1B 3NU

1 2 3 4 5 6 7 8 9 10

✌ PREFACE ❧

This study is intended for students of Spenser. I have not tried to address scholars, though I hope I have not ignored them. In repeating what others have also found in their reading and writing about *The Faerie Queene*, I trust I have not failed to indicate, in the bibliography and notes, many of the places of origin and much of the scope of my debts. Throughout I cite Spenser from *The Complete Poetical Works of Spenser*, ed. R. E. N. Dodge (Boston: Houghton Mifflin Company, 1936).

My hope has been to provide students (and teachers) of Spenser's epic with ways of approaching the poem. The first part of the book is concerned with contexts—the life of Spenser, some forms the epic took before (and after) his own, the pervasiveness of certain literary figures (like Chaucer) and figures from literature (like Arthur) during his time. In discussing these topics, I have also tried to place Spenser's long poem within these contexts and thus introduce the reader to the outlines of my perspective on *The Faerie Queene*.

The second part of the book deals more specifically with Spenser's text itself. The chapter on overall structure, where others have preceded me, is intended to fasten on the whole poem. The next, on Pageantry, is my own foray into the subject and stratagems of Allegory, though I have chosen to speak of Allegory in terms the poem (and not simply the *Letter to Ralegh*) constantly employs. This chapter and the last three then focus on the "play of double senses" (a text derived from Book III, canto iv, stanza 28) as I see it working in specific ways in the epic, thus suggesting how Spenser participates in the epic tradition that I sketched in Chapter II.

I have tried to be responsive to the demands of text and context—hardly a novel critical procedure but one, I hope, that responds to the great English poem as it is also a great Renaissance poem. If I see Proteus and his transforming energies, or the urge to displace marginality with a life at the center of things, as major concerns of *The Faerie Queene*, it is because I also see them as major concerns, expressed in such a variety of ways, in Renaissance literature.

It is with and through my students that I have arrived at many of my conclusions concerning *The Faerie Queene*. And it is to them that this study is dedicated.

A. B. G.

❧ CONTENTS ❧

Part One		1
I.	LIFE OF SPENSER	3
II.	THE FORMS OF EPIC	17
III.	CONTINENTAL AND ENGLISH BACKGROUND TO *THE FAERIE QUEENE*	28
IV.	MUTABILITY AND HEALTH	41
V.	CHAUCER AND SPENSER	47
VI.	ARTHUR: HISTORY AND MYTH	53
Part Two		65
VII.	PATTERNS IN THE POEM	67
VIII.	PAGEANT, SHOW, AND VERSE	78
IX.	INWARD SOUND	94
X.	POETRY AND THE POET	106
XI.	POETS AND PROTEUS	118
NOTES		135
BIBLIOGRAPHY		139

PLAY OF DOUBLE SENSES

SPENSER'S
FAERIE QUEENE

PART ONE

❧ I ☙

LIFE OF SPENSER

We know little of the early life of Edmund Spenser. In the seventy-fourth of the *Amoretti*, his sonnet sequence published in 1595, he tells us his mother's name was Elizabeth, and in the sixtieth, that the year of his courting his lady seems "longer unto me" than all his previous forty. If the sonnets were composed in 1593, as seems likely, then subtracting a year and forty gives 1552 as the probable year of his birth. But it is only a guess. That he was born in London is established in his *Prothalamion* (1596) when he says of the noble brides:

> At length they all to mery London came,
> To mery London, my most kyndly nurse,
> That to me gave this lifes first native sourse,
> Though from another place I take my name,
> An house of auncient fame.
>
> (ll. 127–31)

The "house" Spenser claimed connection with was the Spencers of Althorp and Wormleighton, and there may have been a distant relationship.[1] He never mentions his father, or brothers and sisters, although his father and a brother may both have been named John, and although he did have a sister, Sarah, who married the registrar of the diocese of Cork, Cloyne, and Ross and who stayed with Spenser in Ireland.

We know with certainty that Spenser attended Merchant Taylors' School and then, in 1569, went to Pembroke College, Cambridge. There he took his B.A. in 1573, his M.A. in 1576. We also know that he was always poor and, when still a youth, already a poet. Poor, because he received a gown while at school and small allowances while at Cambridge from a fund set up by the estate of one

3

Robert Nowell. A poet, because among the verses in a relentlessly anti-Catholic tract published in 1569 by a Dutch Calvinist named Jan van der Noot are twenty-two translations from Joachim Du Bellay and (via Clement Marot's French) from Francis Petrarch, done by Spenser.[2] We know they are Spenser's because seventeen of them, in sonnet form, appear among his *Complaints* (1591). Thus at only seventeen or eighteen years old, Spenser had caught the eye of his elders. The money must have been welcome and the (albeit anonymous) taste of printer's ink intoxicating. Judging by what we have and by the nineteen surviving titles of "lost" works, Spenser must have early chosen his path as a poet, and early begun to follow it.[3]

The years at Merchant Taylors' and Cambridge were the formative ones, years of study and growth, and we should pause for a closer look at those institutions during the time Spenser attended them, as well as at some of the extraordinary men under whose influence he came.

On September 24, 1561, in the parish of St. Laurence-Pountney, the Company (or guild) of Merchant Taylors founded a school "for the better educacon & bringing up of Children in good manners & l[iter]ature." [4] The new school's statutes were modeled upon those drawn up by John Colet when he founded St. Paul's in 1509. They provided for an enrollment of 250 "children of all nations & countryes indifferently," 100 who would pay 5s. a quarter, 50 who would pay 2s.2d. and 100 "poore men's sonnes" who would pay nothing. In order to attend, a boy had to be able to say the Catechism in Latin and English and "read perfectly & write competently." Through the plain prose of the statutes, we can glimpse something of a schoolboy's life in one large room not far from the Thames in mid sixteenth-century London.

> The children shall come to the schools in the mornynge at seaven of the clock both winter & somer, & tarry there untill eleaven, & returne againe at one of the clock, and departe at five; and thrice in the day, kneeling on their knees, they shall say the prayers appointed with due tract and pawsing, as they be, or shalbe hereafter conteyned in a table sett up in the schoole, (that is to say) in the morning, at noone, & at evening.

The founders knew the scholars might be hungry, arriving that early, but they were clear on this point:

> Also lett them bring no meate, nor drinck, nor bottles, nor use in the schoole no breakfasts, nor drincking in the tyme of learning in no wise. If they need drinck, then lett it be provided in some other place.

They were equally clear on behavior outdoors:

> Nor lett them use noe cock-fighting, tennys-play, nor riding about of victoring, nor disputing abroade, which is but foolish babling & losse of tyme.

Indeed, the boys could play "only once in a weeke, when there falleth noe holliday" and then on a Tuesday or Thursday afternoon. The founders saw the school as a place of scholarship and moral improvement, and, with Latin at the center of the curriculum (though Greek and Hebrew were also taught), Merchant Taylors' became one of the outstanding schools of the Elizabethan era,[5] along with Westminster, Shrewsbury, and St. Paul's. The school's distinction was due, above all, to its first headmaster, Richard Mulcaster, one of the most extraordinary teachers and thinkers on education of his, or anyone else's, time.

Mulcaster, strict, contentious, stubborn, a stickler for discipline in language and behavior, was born of a Border family in 1530 or 1531, attended Eton, and was a Scholar of King's College, Cambridge, in 1548 and a student at Christ Church, Oxford, in 1555. He was Headmaster of Merchant Taylors' for twenty-five years and Highmaster of St. Paul's from 1596 to 1608. He died in 1611. Mulcaster was renowned for his classical scholarship and his knowledge of Hebrew, but we remember him for his innovative educational theories. These beliefs, set forth in his *Positions* (1581) and *The First Part of the Elementarie* (1582), ranged from his conviction that women should be educated (though not in schools or universities) to his desire for teachers' colleges within the universities.[6]

Mulcaster believed in developing the inclinations and strengths of each individual student; when we remember that he was the teacher of Edmund Spenser, it is interesting to hear him on poets and poetry:

Some vaines be rapt, and will needes proue *poetes,* leaue them the
art of *poetrie,* and the whole bookes and argumentes of *poetes.* Some
will commend to memorie, and posteritie such actes and monumentes
as be worthy the remembrance. (*Positions,* p. 269)

Mulcaster thinks verse is not poetry when written "sadly and
soberly" but is poetry only when poets "couer a truth with a fabulous veele, and resemble with alteration" (*Positions,* p. 269).
Whether because of Mulcaster or not, this is how Spenser will
speak of his poem in the *Letter to Ralegh,* as a "continued allegory
or darke conceit." And certainly the didacticism implicit in this
view of the poet's function emerges clearly in Mulcaster's prose.
For, he goes on, the young poet must learn to shape his language,
as Cicero and Horace did, "to deliuer his minde" (*Positions,* p. 270),
and once the language is well made, it will yield well-formed sentiments, proper to shape the reader.

Moreouer some verie excellent places most eloquently, and forcibly
penned for the polishing of good manners, and inducement vnto
uertue may be picket out of some of them, and none more than
Horace. (*Positions,* p. 270)

We will return later to Spenser's desire through his poem "to
fashion a gentleman or noble person in vertuous and gentle discipline" (*Letter to Ralegh*), but here we may observe how his teacher
preceded him in celebrating the formative power of the teacher or
poet, the user of language.

For the good bring vp of yong gentlemen, he that taketh no care, is
more than a foole considering their place and seruice in our countrie.
(*Positions,* p. 297)

Here, and it is crucial to an understanding of Spenser, is the humanism of Mulcaster, the belief that true education shapes the
private man for the public good. In Chapter III of the *Elementarie,*
on the goal of learning, he brilliantly develops this theme:

For as those, which serue in publik function do turn their learning
to publik vse, which is the naturall vse of all learning: so such as
liue to themselues either for pleasur in their studye, or to avoid foren
truble do turn their learning to a priuate ease, which is the priuat

abuse of a publik good. For the common weall is the measure of everie mans being, which if anie one respect not, he is not to liue in it. (*Elementarie,* pp. 13–14)

This sense of the proper end of education as the formation of a civic being informs all of the *Elementarie*. Every dimension of its stated subject—"reading, writing, drawing, singing, & plaing [of music]" (*Elementarie,* p. 59)—is discussed with an eye to improving the moral health of the individual and, hence, of the commonweal.

There is one other strain in Mulcaster's writings, particularly in the *Elementarie,* that a student of Spenser and of the English Renaissance should note. That is Mulcaster's emphasis on the primacy of English. His humanism and his view of language are allied, for a refined and intelligent use of the native tongue will argue the English "not to be barbarous . . . seing fair speche is som parcell of praise, and a great argument of a well ciuilled people." The proper study of English is also a "helping of vs to foren language" (*Elementarie,* p. 56), but later Mulcaster will recommend English for reasons other than civility and utility. He praises English, "a tung of it self both depe in conceit, & frank in deliuerie," for its flexibility and variety.

I do not think that anie language, be it whatsoeuer, is better able to vtter all arguments, either with more pith, or greater planesse, than our *English* tung is, if the *English* vtterer be as skilfull in the matter, which he is to vtter. (*Elementarie,* p. 274)

This linguistic patriotism asserts itself powerfully through the *Elementarie*—it is as much a part of Mulcaster's personality as his love of order or his psychological shrewdness.

I love *Rome,* but *London* better, I fauor *Italie,* but England more, I honor Latin, but I worship the English. (*Elementarie,* p. 269)

We will return more than once to this love of language and land, and to what it will mean to Spenser and others.

On May 20, 1569, Spenser arrived at Pembroke College, Cambridge, and began the stay that would end seven years later. He was a Sizar, that is a scholarship student, and therefore entitled to free board, room, and tuition in return for performing such duties

as waiting on table, working in the kitchen, or aiding the Master or
Fellows. As set forth in the revised University statutes of 1570, the
routine of the student's day began with chapel at five in the morn-
ing, with the rest of the day concerned with public lectures and
disputations and study, the gates of the college then closing at eight
in the evening in winter, nine in summer.[7] The colleges enforced
strict regulations concerning dress, offered much religious instruc-
tion, and encouraged a careful separation from the surrounding
town and fairs. This last, not simply because of the natural tendency
of town and gown to beat each other up, and not only to keep the
scholars from the manifold delights of loitering, cards, and bearbaiting—but also because of the plague. Between July 24 and
November 21, 1574, plague carried off 115 persons in Cambridge,
not one of them a student.

Religious disputes between Puritans and those loyal to the established Church, and the wooing of Elizabeth by French representa-
tives of the duke of Anjou, must have engaged Spenser's attention,
as they did everyone else's. And he must have pursued the course
for the B.A. as provided by statute: in the first year, lectures on
grammar and rhetoric, by way of Quintilian, Hermogenes, and
Cicero's *Orations*; in the second and third, logic, by way of Aristotle
and Cicero; philosophy, with lectures on Aristotle (*Ethics, Politics,
and Problems*), Pliny, and Plato. And for the M.A., more of the
same, with drawing, astronomy (the old law of Ptolemy), and Greek
(Homer, Isocrates, Demosthenes, and others). As Judson says, an
Elizabethan University education was all classical:

> . . . of the eighteen authors prescribed for the University lectures in
> all fields, including law and medicine . . . Only two of these authors
> lived later than the second century of our era—Girolamo Cardano and
> Bishop Tunstall, Renaissance scholars who wrote on arithmetic. (*Life,*
> p. 27)

A glance at the catalogs of 1556/7, 1573, and 1574 for the Cambridge University Library will confirm this observation. All three
catalogs list works only in Greek and Latin. Among the many
dictionaries, codices, commentaries, sermons, and tracts are substantial collections of the Church Fathers, of historians from Herodotus
and Thucydides to Livy and Josephus, and, in all three catalogs, the

same poets: Homer, Lucan, Apollonius of Rhodes, Valerius Flaccus, Statius, Plautus, and Terence. This last lay on the shelf next to the *Summa Theologica* of St. Thomas Aquinas. The only "modern" book of remotely literary interest is the copy (bound with something else) of Francis Petrarch's letters.[8] As we will see, however, the view of a University education provided by requirements and catalogs was not necessarily any more accurate then than now.

During his Cambridge years and until 1580, Spenser's closest friend and intellectual companion was Gabriel Harvey. Handsome, ambitious, scholarly, genuinely learned in the ancient and modern languages, Harvey was also, as Judson puts it, "tactless, egotisticall, arrogant, vain" (*Life*, p. 37). Born around 1550 to a wealthy rope maker and farmer in Saffron-Walden, Harvey studied at Christ College, Cambridge, was elected Fellow of Pembroke in 1570, for a while was denied his M.A. by his colleagues there, later became a Doctor of Laws, authored four Latin treatises on philosophy and rhetoric, conducted (to his disadvantage) savage polemics with Thomas Nashe, and died an old and disappointed man in 1630. All his life Harvey craved preferment and great fame, but today he is chiefly remembered because he was Spenser's friend. The published letters between them talk most of their attempts to impose classical rules of quantity (long and short vowels) upon English verse, according to the rules laid down by Bishop Thomas Drant.[9] But they are also interesting for what they can tell us of Cambridge and the reading of a University man of the time.

In a letter of April 7, 1580, Harvey says, ". . . what Newes all this while at Cambridge?"

Tully and *Demosthenes* nothing so much studied, as they were wont: *Liuie* and *Salust* possiblye rather more, than lesse: *Lucian* never so much: Aristotle much named, but litle read: *Xenephon* and *Plato*, reckned amongest Discoursers, and conceited Superficiall fellowes: much verball and Sophisticall iangling: little subtile and effectuall disputing: . . . . *Matchiavell* a great man: *Castilio* [Baldassare Castiglione, author of *Il Cortegiano*, translated by Sir Thomas Hoby as *The Courtier*, 1561] of no small reputation: *Petrarch* and *Boccace* in euery mans mouth: *Galateo* [courtesy book after Castiglione's, by Giovanni della Casa] and *Guazzo* [Stefano Guazzo, author of the courtesy book *Civil Conversatione*] never so happy: over many ac-

quainted with *Vnico Aretio* [Bernardo Accolti, improvisor of Pe-
trarchan verse at Urbino]: The French and Italian when so highly re-
garded of Schollars? The Latine and Greeke, when so lightly? (*Works*,
I, 69)

In a letter in his private "letter-book," Harvey says much the same
thing—"Aristotles Organon is nigh as litle redd as Dunses [Duns
Scotus'] Quodlibet,"—and he names many of the same Italian authors, and more in French, to show the degeneration of learning.
Interestingly, however, he shows a wide knowledge of what he de-
plores, mentioning, to pick only one author, not only Machiavelli's
"parlous byoke" *The Prince*, but also the Florentine's *Art of War*,
Discourses, and *History of Florence* (*Works*, I, 137–38). Whatever
his tone, Harvey and those like him, including Spenser, were well
acquainted with the latest lights of the Continent.

All this, and much more, Spenser imbibed at Cambridge and in
the years immediately following. He must have read widely during
his year as secretary to John Taylor, Bishop of Rochester (who had
been the Master of Pembroke during his stay) in 1579. And Spenser
read and undoubtedly wrote much in 1579 to 1580 when he was in
London as part of the circle of Robert Dudley, earl of Leicester,
the arrogant, impressive favorite of the Queen. Here he knew
Leicester's glittering nephew, Sir Philip Sidney, the "glass of fashion
and mold of form" to an age, and the poet Edward Dyer and others.
And here, among the great, Spenser's never-to-be-satisfied appetite
for position and preferment (a hunger he shared with Harvey and
countless others) was whetted. But while he impatiently awaited
employment in Leicester's service, he probably married, on October
27, 1579, his first wife, thought to be named Machabyas Childe, and
he wrote or polished many of his "lost" works. We know that in that
year he published, anonymously, his great sequence of pastoral
poems, *The Shepheardes Calender*. In these twelve "months" or
poems, Spenser assumes the name Colin Clout, the name by which
he will figure himself in all his subsequent poetry. The poems flay
ecclesiastical corruption and celebrate the lovely and unobtainable
Rosalind, and they bring the Renaissance to England.

There is an elaborate apparatus to *The Shepheardes Calender*—
a dedicatory epistle to Harvey, a "generall argument of the whole

booke," arguments, as well as emblems or mottoes, to the individual
months, and elaborate notes. All this is the work of one "E. K."—
probably Edmund Kirke, a contemporary of Spenser's at Cambridge
and later a clergyman. However, although there is no way of proving it, my own strong feeling is that the whole apparatus may have
been the collaborative effort of Spenser, Harvey, and "E. K.," errors,
fatuities, and all; or, at least, that Spenser and Harvey knew very
well what was being said, for the mixture of puffery, academic
parody, and coterie winking, in addition to the genuine learning,
seems very much in the bookish, witty-solemn spirit of Cambridge.
If we examine the epistle, arguments, and glosses of the *Calender*,
as well as other poems, we can form a better idea of the authors
Spenser read, of the books that nourished him. In what follows, I
do not claim to be in any sense exhaustive, either of what Spenser
alludes to or of what he would be assumed to have read; I only
want to indicate the kinds of authors we know he looked in. The
list is meant to be descriptive.[10]

Among the ancients, one finds allusions to or citations of the
philosophers Plato, Aristotle, and Xenephon (as a philosopher in
LR); historians Ennius (*Ded. Son.* I), Livy, Sallust, Tacitus, Dio-
dorus Siculus, and Eusebius. Cicero is cited often and Macrobius
at least once. Of the poets, allusions to Homer's epics (*LR*) and
Virgil's *Eclogues, Georgics,* and *Aeneid* of course appear, as do
allusions to Hesiod, the pastoralists Theocritus and Moschus, and
Terence, Horace, Ovid, Propertius, Seneca, and Lucian.

Of Renaissance writers on the Continent, we know Spenser translated Du Bellay and Petrarch (through Marot's French); Marot is
mentioned often in the *Calender* apparatus ("November" is mod-
elled on an elegy of Marot's), and Harvey tells us Spenser was particularly fond of "the fourth day of the first weeke of [Du]Bartas." [11]
Of the Italians cited in the *Calender* in addition to Petrarch, we
find Boccaccio, Poliziano, and Sannazaro, and in the *Letter to
Ralegh* Spenser alludes to his great favorites, Ariosto and Tasso.
Of works written in Latin, glosses to the *Calender* note the eclogues
of Mantuan and the *Adages* of Erasmus.[12]

The English poets were closest to him. As we will see, Spenser
was devoted to Chaucer. E. K. refers to Lydgate; John Skelton pro-

vided the name Colin Clout. In the "letter-book," Harvey says
Spenser "could very wel abide [George] Gascoignes Steele glasse"
(*Works,* I, 180), which we could gather as well from the warm men-
tion of Gascoigne in the gloss to "Philomele" in "November."
Of his contemporaries, Spenser figures the poets Michael Drayton as
Aetion (*CCCHA,* 444) and Thomas Churchyard as Palaemon
(*CCCHA,* 346); he alludes to Samuel Daniel's *Complaint to Rosa-
mund* and *Delia* (*CCCHA,* 427; 418) and to Thomas Watson's
Meliboeus (*RT,* 436). He writes a dedicatory sonnet to Thomas
Sackville, Lord Buckhurst, author of the *Induction* to *The Mirror
for Magistrates,* a poem whose style he must eagerly have absorbed.
Sir Philip Sidney's *Astrophel and Stella* is noted (*CCCHA,* 534) as is
William Alabaster's *Eliseïs* (*CCCHA,* 403) and his good friend
Ralegh's *Ocean to Cynthia* (*F.Q.* III, proem 4, and *CCCHA,* 428–
31). There are others—probably John Lyly at *TM,* 217–22, and the
great historian and antiquarian William Camden, "nourrice of
antiquitie," at *RT,* 169—but the point is that even though he was
in Ireland for most of his adult life, Spenser was abreast of the
literature of his time.

He was steeped in other books as well, and scholars have adduced
a vast array of "sources" and "influences" that affected Spenser, as a
glance at the *Variorum* edition will often show. Surely he knew the
Bible more thoroughly than anything else, as well as the medieval
allegorical tradition as best outlined by Rosamund Tuve, the philo-
sophical sources noted by J. E. Hankin, the mythographers cited by
Talbot and Starnes and by Bush, and many other poets and writers
whose impression one can see in his verse. (For references, see
Bibliography at the end.) My intention, however, is not to track
influences, but rather to describe the kind of reading Spenser did;
and lest we think all was unrelieved solemnity, that a sixteenth-
century poet was incapable of "light" reading, we will close this
little survey of education and reading by noting two gifts Spenser
made in 1578 to Harvey. One was a copy of *The Traveiler of Ierome
Turler* (1575), a lively book of travel information and misinforma-
tion, including a description of corrupt Naples of the kind the
Elizabethans liked so much (see a similar kind of passage near the
beginning of Lyly's *Euphues*). From Harvey's inscription in the
Traveiler, we know that Spenser was secretary to the Bishop of

Rochester. Harvey describes the other gift and its purpose in his copy of one of the four books:

This Howletglasse, with Skoggin, Skelton, and L[a]zarillo, giuen me at London, of Mr. Spenser xx Decembris [15]78 on condition [that I] shoold bestowe ye reading of them oue[r] before ye first of January [imme]diately ensuing: otherwise to forfeit unto him my Lucian in four uolumes.[13]

We catch something of the slyness of Spenser who, badly wanting the Lucian, knew what a painful chore he was setting his pedantic friend. Harvey complains that he lost many hours reading Spenser's four books. The *Howleglass* is the adventures of Til Eulenspiegel, *Skoggin* and *Skelton* are jestbooks, and Lazarillo [de Tormes] is the famous Spanish picaresque novel. Spenser obviously had a taste for books of wandering and adventure in foreign lands, and in 1580 he commenced his own sojourn in a distant land, one which, save for short visits and to come home to die, would last the rest of his life.

On August 12, 1580, Spenser arrived in Dublin. He had become secretary to the Lord Deputy for Ireland, Arthur Lord Grey de Wilton, probably with help from the Sidney circle. He now began his long career as a civil servant to Her Majesty's government in Ireland, a career that would see him travel throughout the lovely land, accompanying Lord Grey and his successors on their missions to bolster allies, quell rebellions, mete out justice—a story told in Book V of *The Faerie Queene*. Spenser learned to love the rivers, bogs, woods, and mountains of Ireland and to hate her people, the starving peasantry and the proud, devious Anglo-Irish nobility.[14] In 1581, he assumed the clerkship in Chancery for faculties, which meant he oversaw ecclesiastical licenses and dispensations, and he held that post until 1588. In 1582, Lord Grey left his post, frustrated by Elizabeth's refusal properly to supply an army, and by the dissension and civil strife of the country. At this time, Spenser acquired New Abbey, a house near Kilcullen on the Liffey, twenty-five miles south of Dublin and in sight of the great Bog of Allen, where gnats would rise "as a cloud doth seeme to dim the skies" (*F.Q.*, II,ix,16). He stayed at New Abbey from 1582 to 1584, enjoying the company of the literary men Lodowick Bryskett, Barnabe Rich, and Barnaby

Googe, and writing *The Faerie Queene.* In the summer of 1584, Spenser became deputy to the Clerk of Council, Munster, and his fortunes became even more closely tied to that richest and southern-most of the divisions of Ireland.

His family was growing—a son, Sylvanus, was born sometime be-fore 1582, and perhaps a daughter Katherine—and he had found the life of a gentleman-farmer congenial, so between late 1588 and spring of 1589, he acquired Kilcolman, an estate of 3,028 acres mid-way between Limerick and Cork. In order to repopulate Munster, the Government was offering lands to "undertakers" who would bring in English families and begin to restore the land. It was pro-vided that twenty-four families, including his own, would settle and work his land. And there was also a fascinating neighbor, for thirty miles away was Lismore Castle, belonging to Sir Walter Ralegh, and to the east was Ralegh's 42,000-acre estate of Inchiquin. Ralegh and Spenser probably knew each other in 1579; now, in 1589, Ralegh visited Spenser and the two poets read to each other, and discussed, their poetry. Spenser's epic had grown. It was time to return. Ralegh accompanied Spenser back to London in 1589 and on December 1, Books I–III of *The Faerie Queene* were entered in the Stationer's Register. Spenser found that he had not been for-gotten. The *Calender* had had new editions in 1581 and 1586, and in 1588, Abraham Fraunce had cited, in his *Arcadian Rhetoricke,* Book II, canto iv, stanza 35, of *The Faerie Queene,* with the name of its author. Word had preceded him. Returning was not at all unpleasant.

Very quickly, Spenser wrote his *Letter to Raleigh,* setting forth the plan and principles of his long poem, as the preface to *The Faerie Queene*; composed seventeen dedicatory sonnets as well; and saw to the printing of the first three books of the epic in early 1590. By May he was back in Ireland, but he returned again to Elizabeth's court. The desire for patronage, position, and reward was powerful. And even more, much as he loathed the superficialities of the court and missed his land of rivers, this was the center of the civility he valued, this was the glorious clearing at the center of the wood where the Faery Queen lived. He stayed on. In 1591, the *Calender* had another edition, the *Complaints* were published, and finally in

February, 1591, he was granted an annuity of fifty pounds. It had been a long time coming and there are many legends concerning the enmity of William Cecil, Lord Burghley, Elizabeth's canny Lord Treasurer, toward Spenser. Certainly in various of the poems in the *Complaints* the poet is bitter about his neglect.[15]

He went home. On June 11, 1594, he was married for a second time, to Elizabeth Boyle, a union that would produce a son, Peregrine. Their courtship is celebrated in the *Amoretti*. More poems followed: *Colin Clouts Come Home Againe,* the *Amoretti,* and *Epithalamion* were published in 1595, and in the winter of that year Spenser was back in London. In 1596, Books I–VI were brought out, IV–VI being added to the 1590 edition of I–III, a fusion that meant the suppression of the original ending of Book III and the addition of a new one. His *Fowre Hymnes* and *Prothalamion* were also published in that year. In the late autumn of 1596, Spenser was back in Ireland, which was about to undergo its worst upheaval of Elizabeth's reign.

Far in the north, Hugh O'Neill, third baron of Dungannon and second earl of Tyrone, was preparing the fire. It broke out in June of 1598, and on August 19, the Queen's forces were routed at the Battle of the Yellow Ford near Armagh. In October, some 2,000 rebels blazed across Leinster into Munster, and that rich area, populated by new English tenants and by Irish openly sympathetic to the rebels, did not long resist. Spenser's "fair stone house" was burned. In the Irish State papers for October, 1598, we read that "Edmund [MacSheehy] was killed by an Englishman at the spoil of Kilcolman." [16] Was that Englishman Spenser? There is no way of knowing, any more than we know if Spenser, fleeing to Cork with his family and the other English settlers, was aware that on September 30 the Privy Council had urged the Lord Justices in Dublin to appoint him High Sheriff of that city. The long desired preferment had arrived. Too late.

On the day before Christmas, 1598, Spenser brought letters from officials in Ireland to Elizabeth's court in Whitehall. Just three weeks later, on January 13, 1599, in Westminster, he died. A decade later, Ben Jonson told Drummond of Hawthornden that after the Irish robd Spensers goods, and burnt his house and a little child new born, he and his wyfe escaped, and after, he died for lake of bread in King Street, and refused 20 pieces sent to him by my Lord of Essex, and said, He was sorrie he had no time to spend them.

Whether or not the baby was Spenser's will never be known, but the outline of his last days as given by Jonson agrees with the account offered in 1615 by the great Camden in his history of the life and reign of Elizabeth:

> . . . he was cast forth of doores by the Rebels, and robbed of his goods, and sent ouer very poore into *England*, where presently after hee dyed; and was buried at *Westminster* neere *Chawcer*, at the charges of the Earle of *Essex*, all Poets carrying his body to Church, and casting their dolefull Verses, and Pens too in his grave.[17]

With this last pageant, the long exile was over. The search for power or reward, for some mark of the world's recognition, had come to rest at the center of the city he loved, supported by the mighty, surrounded by his brother poets. The end of exile at the edges, the search for some core of value at the center of the wilderness of our existence, these and other urges grew out of his life and became the themes of his art. We shall see them over and over in *The Faerie Queene*. But before we can look at that epic achievement we must, as Spenser did, go the long way around.

❧ II ❧

THE FORMS OF EPIC

> Names, deeds, grey legends, dire events, rebellions,
> Majesties, sovran voices, agonies,
> Creations and destroyings, all at once
> Pour into the wide hollow of my brain.
>
> (Keats, *Hyperion*, III, 114–17)

In the third book of the *Aeneid*, Aeneas tells Dido and her court of the Trojan disaster and how finally he and his men reached Buthrotum, a Greek city ruled by Priam's son Helenus and his consort, Andromache, Hector's widow. In Aeneas' account, we learn a fundamental lesson of the poem: One must rid oneself of the past in order to build the future. Buthrotum was meant to be a replica of Troy in every detail, but the brook intended to duplicate the Simois is dry and the tomb of Hector where Andromache worships and weeps is empty. Everywhere we see the sadness and futility, the melancholy sterility, of living in and living off the past. With Aeneas, we learn to look forward, not back; forward to the new city, the new hope—not another Troy, not even a new Carthage, but Rome. With the hero, we fix on that high walled place where, as Anchises tells his son in the depths of Book VI, the fine arts will be "to rule nations, to crown peace with law / And to spare the conquered and to conquer the proud" (VI, 851–53). "Sic pater Anchises." So said the father.

So said the father, who is a central figure in epic, whether he is called Jove or Priam or Anchises or Charlemagne or God. So the father, who gives us life, teaches us to live together. And in revealing this civilizing impulse through the father, these large, public, historically oriented poems unfold their massive subject: man's effort to impose civilization within and without himself, his desire and need to earn citizenship in a city of man or of God. So the father

17

tells the son in the Underworld, that deep, dark place in the self where the roots of the self begin, and so the son learns to be a father, to his people, to his city, to himself.

This view forward, however, that reveals the glories of the civilized life and that justifies the process whereby fathers make fathers of their sons, is not the only view epic offers. There is also the view back, toward the ruined city of Troy that, like Priam, slipped in its own blood. This is the view not of what we should or must be but of what we have been and are. If epics justify the ways of fathers to sons, they also reveal the ways of sons to fathers, the explosive, anarchic ways in which new growth means forcible tearing and sundering from the old. This view back sees how death, decay, and desolation underlie all our best hopes. And so one notices in epic poems the constant sense that what we create and build—selves, families, cities—will always be prey to time and change, for what can escape? What city, what Troy or Athens, Rome or London, can last? Every epic poet who knows how glorious Troy was also knows that its fate will come to us all.

One can say the epic is a profoundly political kind of poem, if we take *political* as it is derived from the Greek *polis,* city, and thus is concerned with the way men live in community. But we mistake this political preoccupation if we regard epic only as celebrating creation and hymning the order and goodly government of things. Epic does sing of order, but out of necessity as much as delight; for epic is profoundly aware of the forces that destroy, of the disease and savage loneliness within man that renders so much of his human effort futile. The *Iliad,* after all, ends with the imminent destruction of a city; the festive *Odyssey* culminates with a vast feast hall littered with dead bodies. And the *Aeneid* begins with Troy in flames and ends with another city conquered, as, in the name of fatherhood and civilization, Aeneas becomes another Achilles, and brutal Turnus another Hector, killed before a conquered town. *Paradise Lost,* for all the hopes and promises of redemption, ends with the solitary pair wandering past flaming swords, exiled from the garden that was a perfect earthly image of God's city. The great civilizing passage of the son to fatherhood, of the individual to an institution, cannot be accomplished without pain and loss. "For nothing can be sole or whole," says Yeats, "that has not been rent."

In many ways, great epics illuminate man's need and man's in-capacity to control the demonic and destructive forces within him and around him. Great epics all celebrate what man can make, and the poem itself is the chief image of that power. But these very poems also tell of the futility of man's efforts to subdue and contain the same potent forces he has tapped. We will return more than once to that mystery at the heart of epic, to that mix or mingle of the creative and destructive, of growth and decay, of order and monstrosity. We will examine often the way epic probes that basic human dilemma, whereby love and hate are fed by the same nerve, whereby the forces of life are also the agents of death. We cannot escape the epic's focus on the way we obey the law of fatherhood while denying what is best in the father we love.

I

"Quidve sequens tantos possim superare labores?" (*Aeneid* III, 368) So Aeneas at Buthrotum asked his host Helenus, who is a seer: "By what course can I overcome such suffering?" *Labores,* the Vir-gilian *labor,* effort, work, the expenditure of energy: Here the great word (and virtue) carries a note of travail and weariness. Aeneas is asking: How can I get home? What must I do? What will it cost me in terms of myself? What is it going to take to establish stability? These are the questions epics always ask. But the basic question in epic, because these poems always "know" where they are going, is: How do we get there? Thus the old idea of epic as a quest, a seeking in the world—to destroy Troy or to found Rome, to defeat the In-fidel for King and Cross, find the Grail, free Jerusalem, see the face of God, discover India or Peru, worship at the court of the glorious Faery Queene. The idea of the quest is a basic and useful one. From another perspective, however, epics are equally about exile, for the quest is often to get home, to get back to those roots where one lives at harmony with oneself. The quest is the search for where we began, the end of our exile from what we love: in the *Odyssey,* our exile from Ithaca and Penelope; in the *Iliad,* the exile from Helen, for that is why they go to Troy; our exile from Beatrice and God, in Dante's *Comedy*; our exile from Elizabeth and her court, in Spenser's *Faerie Queene.*

The epic is often concerned with exile and the way back, and woman is always at the center. She is often both the goal and the obstacle. She is Penelope who waits and Circe who delays. She is Dido, who slows us, and Rome—Roma, the feminine place—who calls us on. Sometimes she is both the reason we wander and the object we seek, because only where she is are we at home. Such a woman is Helen, or Eve, Eve who causes our exile from the Garden and from the Father, and Eve with whom we find a new homestead and by whose sons we become fathers ourselves. Always obeying the law of paternity, defying the father who loves us.

We come back to the center of epic, that core of experience where our humanity is defined by the contradictions it encompasses. We return to that heart of the epic where our urge to be reconciled in harmony is the same urge that tears us into solitary fragments. But whether we see epic as emphasizing quest or exile, the impulse to go out and make cities, or to go home and rest; whether we stress the contradictory nature of fatherhood, or womanhood—in short, whether we opt for the specific focus of the *Iliad* or that of the *Odyssey* (and finally they are always mixed), we are taught that all human enterprise and endeavor involve a long, weary way. That to get *there* means going a long, long distance, a long space in time. We cannot escape epic's long view: that rest will come by never resting, that peace will come only by war, that all your future will be devoted, despite yourself and at best, to finding a memory from the past.

And so Helenus, inspired by Apollo, tells Aeneas how he must go, where to stop, what to avoid. When you see Scylla and Charybdis, he says, Scylla a maiden above, a monster below—again, the inexplicable, double image of woman in the midst of the journey—when you see her, better double back, and, lingering, fetch a double compass, "circumflectere cursus." Better, in short, go the long way around. And this long way around is precisely the way he goes and is the way all epic moves, as the poem itself charts for the reader the course that the poem describes. The epic poem, oblique, indirect, always digressive, interpolating tales, pausing for breath—the poet's, the hero's, ours—is itself always moving towards its own goal, its own completed fixity and revealed pattern. Yet while the poem is going home, so to speak, it seems as aimless as we are in our lives.

It seems always to choose the long way around, which is finally the only way, as every poet and every man knows for himself. He "winds with ease / Through the pure marble Air his oblique way," and later:

> With tract oblique
> At first, as one who sought access but feared
> To interrupt, side-long he works his way.

So in *Paradise Lost* Milton describes Satan, as escaped fiend in Book III, as subtle snake in Book IX. But Milton also describes the way his poem works, the way he works as a poet, and the way all epics and their poets work.

Often we grow impatient with epic poems. Too long, we feel—all those irrelevant interruptions, those additions, conventions, invocations, interpolations, those stories and speeches, catalog and dull history. But these are all part of the journey, the reader's journey on his long way around. For just as there are epic poets, involved in the task of creating, and just as there are epic heroes, who labor to create, so also are there epic readers. And all those digressions and history and stretches of catalog, all those elements of the poem which image the vastness and variety of the real world, allow the epic poet to involve the epic reader in the meaning of the poem, which is the immense difficulty of getting *there* and the driving necessity to go. The great length of the epic, the vast meandering, is meant to communicate the laborious and perhaps futile effort of the hero and poet to master all the stuff of history and experience. For whether one is an epic protagonist caught in the massive world of contingency, or the epic poet trying to bring order from the chaos of mankind's memories, or the epic reader trying to get through the long poem, in each case one is attempting to limit the seemingly limitless, striving to control and master the seemingly endless. The reader's confrontation with the huge poem imitates the epic hero's confrontation with his vast world, and in both cases man's need for control and his need for completion are stretched to their utmost.

The long way around or digressive techniques of epic also serve another purpose. By lingering or pausing or turning back, the epic poet includes an immense amount in order to image the apparently endless complexity we humans must face. But the poet also proceeds obliquely so he will have enough room for his historical concerns. The epic poet's problem is that he must have enough space for all of time. His historical concerns come in many forms, but whatever they are, secular or divine, national, social, or individual, or all of these at once, the poet often focuses on another kind of history as well. He often focuses on literary history; for, particularly by the Renaissance, literary history is a fundamental concern and basic tool of the poet. In the Renaissance, epic is not only the queen of the genres; it is also the most literary genre.

Epic poets are immensely concerned with other epic poems; that is, a given poet is constantly and overtly looking over his shoulder at his predecessors' poems. For instance, in a letter to Spenser, Gabriel Harvey says he thinks Spenser's (now lost) *Nine Comedies* no more approach Ariosto's than "that *Eluish Queene* doth to his *Orlando Furioso,* which notwithstanding, you wil needes seeme to emulate, and hope to overgo, as you flatly professed yourself in one of your last letters" (Grosart, *Works,* I, 95). If Spenser, in a letter now lost, did flatly profess his desire to emulate and to "overgo" the *Orlando Furioso* with his *Faerie Queene,* then he was simply responding to his great predecessor in the habitual fashion of epic poets. Ariosto had hoped to overgo Boiardo, whose unfinished poem Ariosto took up and continued; Boiardo, as he makes clear, intended to unify and thus supersede all the *chansons de geste* about Charlemagne, on the one hand, and the Arthurian romances that he had inherited from the middle ages, on the other. Of course, Virgil is the model, for the Renaissance clearly recognized that the first six books of the *Aeneid* are an *Odyssey,* the second six an *Iliad.* It is the deepest desire of the epic poet to overgo his forerunners in the art; we see this best with Milton, who surpassed them all.

At *Paradise Lost,* I, 16, Milton announces the aim of his "adventurous Song" to pursue "Things unattempted yet in Prose or Rhyme." When we hear this grand vaunt, we are thrilled. And we are no less thrilled when we realize that Ariosto begins the *Orlando Furioso* with precisely the same words (I,ii) and that Boiardo begins the *Orlando Innamorato* substantially the same way (I,i,1)—all in imitation of Horace in the First Ode of Book Three. Nor is our pleasure in Milton's boast diminished when we find that Spenser,

Faerie Queene, VI, proem, 2, and Dante, *Divine Comedy, Paradise,* II, 6, also said the same thing. Nothing is more traditional than the claim to be making an innovation. The point is that we are expected to know the claim has been made before. From the poet's point of view, we *must* know of the boast's previous existence, else we will not recognize the significance of the most recent poet's achievement. Epic poems, ever since Antiquity the noblest form of poetry, for which the high style was reserved, must contain and include all that went before; and that means all previous encyclopaedic efforts at inclusion, all previous epic poems. Thus Renaissance poets ennoble their matter by consciously surpassing previous literary images of nobility. One sense in which epics are literarily self-conscious is their view of themselves as inheritors and containers of previous epic literature.

The reason the epic seeks to store previous literature emerges when we consider the epic poet's immense task: to sum up a vision of the society or history or condition of man at his largest and best. With all human history at stake, through individuals or through a nation, the task of including man's creations and aspirations and failures becomes more difficult the more there is. However, if epics in particular or literature in general distill the essence of a time or belief, of a culture or society, then by referring to literature, we can make reference to life. If we believe the *Aeneid* contains those values Rome esteemed most, then we can refer to those values—patriotic, religious, communal, legal—by taking the long way around and implicating, involving, borrowing from, echoing, and alluding to the *Aeneid.* Thus literary history can be made an analogue to human history. To refer within your epic to other epics is to create and sustain a shorthand by which you refer to all that came before. By this shorthand, the poet proves that his patron or nation or language, his values and culture, his poem, is superior because it knows, and can include, all that came before, all there is to know. To satisfy their encyclopaedic thrust, epic poems include and exploit previous literature as the only way of storing previous life.

In its quest for completeness epic stores within itself all kinds of literature. What A. S. P. Woodhouse has said of *The Faerie Queene* can be said of most great epic poems of the Renaissance:

> There is scarcely a genre that it does not involve or draw on—epic
> narrative, chivalric quest, the whole range of allegorical poetry . . .
> not to mention pastoral, emblem, idyll, interlude and masque.[1]

The list might even be extended, but Mr. Woodhouse's point is well
made. Epic inclusiveness is just that—the urge to know and absorb
all forms of experience. Thus, to include forms of experience, epic
includes literary forms; to contain all kinds of life, it contains all the
kinds of literature. Each of these literary kinds, or genres, has a
different type of psychic appeal; each literary kind summons and
involves a different level of the mind, a different set of reactions, a
different pattern of feeling. Each brings to bear on human activity
a different perspective. And all these different ways of seeing, in
their cunning juxtaposition and arrangement, bring new insight,
new versions of vision.

Thus the epic reader is forced to correct his sight, adjust his gaze,
and absorb new or renewed experience, for the very act of reading
the epic poem, with its multiple versions of human reality, its various literary kinds, is itself a new experience. Epic becomes what it
describes: It embodies the varieties of literature in order to display
life's various modes. Epic literature, either as the various genres in
careful array or as the whole called epic narrative, is thus constantly
urging us to take it seriously as a way of stretching and radically re-
forming the mind.

II

My emphasis on the literary self-conscious of Renaissance epic
may create the impression that Renaissance poets were mistaking art
for life and were substituting the appearance of things as created by
art for the reality of life as created by God. Did the Renaissance
poet in fact think he was God? No, but he saw himself like God—
Spenser says a "godlike man" (IV,ii,1)—omniscient, omnipotent, the
creator of plenitude and variety, a maker (that old word for poet)
of a micro-cosmos. However, no Renaissance poet ever proposed that
fiction is reality. Indeed, the final sense in which we can speak of the
Renaissance epic's literary self-consciousness is the sense poets had of
their epics' status as *poems,* as artifacts, as things—to adapt Tasso's

words—"made," not "born" (*Gerusalemme Liberata,* XIV, 48). Renaissance poets knew better than anyone that their powers were only God-like, and not God's. They well knew that their poems were only images of reality, not the thing itself. And like other forms of knowledge, they included this knowledge in their poems. Renaissance epics become virtually obsessed with the problems of art and nature, illusion and reality; they constantly examine the deceitfulness of appearances, and return again and again to the creation of fictions, myths, conventions, codes, constructs, artifacts.

Epic poems of the Renaissance are concerned with the imposition of order to create new versions of life; that is, they are in a sense concerned with poetry. But these epics are themselves such versions of experience, such illusions of reality—and if one of the lessons they teach is that words, fictions, appearances are misleading or dangerous, then how can we trust the very poem that conveys this message? The poems become instances of the problem they propose to examine. They are creations in language that warn against the power of words. In short, Renaissance epics often teach us not to trust Renaissance epics. They force us back towards life, civic and active; they urge us to learn, by reading, how to live—not how to substitute books for the world.

We see this thrust everywhere: in Ariosto's concern to show how the codes and conventions of chivalry are fictions we create to gull ourselves into believing the world is working the way we want it to; in Spenser's constant warnings against taking what appears for what is; above all, in Cervantes' great book *Don Quixote,* whose fundamental preoccupation is books. After all the emphasis in poetry on the fallibility and instability of language, Cervantes' great swan song of chivalric romance in the Renaissance takes as its subject a man who mistakes poems for life, literary epics for real experience. Cervantes' book carries the epic's literary self-consciousness to its logical conclusion and, among other things, is about the power of illusion and language to destroy. *Don Quixote* virtually begins with a scene in which many of the books upon which *Don Quixote* is based are burned (I,vi). As the housekeeper, niece, barber, and priest preside over the Inquisition and consign the offending books to the flames in the courtyard below, we have the most graphic image in

Renaissance literature for the destructive impulses in Renaissance literature. Here the seeds in epic that contained the destruction of epic are allowed to flower, paradoxically in a book most memorable for the elements it sought to extinguish.

So, the twin impulses of epic: to show man imposing order, while conveying the futility of trying to control chaos; to show the foundation of cities, while taking us across space and times littered with decayed cities and with human landscapes where the "mansion of mortality," the "castle of health," as Spenser says, is dying and diseased. As the epic proposes limitless horizons against which man must raise limits, and implies that the effort may be for nought, so the epic before Milton (for *Paradise Lost* is the exception in many ways) is a creation aware always of its own fallibility. It is an illusion warning against appearances; it is made of words ever whispering, precisely amidst the glories and virtues they conjure, not to trust conjurers—not to trust anything save God, who is unavailable save by faith.

The epic poet of the Renaissance, who had to know everything, knew too much. He knew, as Spenser knew and says in so many ways, that art can bind up the wounds of time; words can freeze change into something eternal; poems can move out of time, for all time. But he also knew art was not life, or true pleasure, or real virtue, but only a painted scene, and that to mistake what seems for what is would be to commit the error his poem warns against. Since the Fall there is no perfection save in art, and that is superb but not, finally, true.

As we read *The Faerie Queene,* we will note the poet's preoccupation with the power to fictionalize. We will see him creating his own myths as he struggles to contain mutability. We will note how the tone of the poem darkens and deepens as we go the long way around until, at the end, in Book VI, a poet-shepherd named Colin Clout, who figured Spenser himself in the *Shepheardes Calender* and *Colin Clouts Come Home Againe,* conjures a vision of perfect stillness and motion, symmetry and grace, in the dancing ladies on Mount Acidale. Colin conjures only to have the vision shattered by the intrusion of Calidore, knight of Courtesy, hero of Book VI. Spenserian irony abounds as he who is eager to partake of this vision causes it to disappear; he who is bursting with benign and wholesome intentions destroys the last image of perfection in the poem. In that shattered vision on Mount Acidale, we will see a version of the epic impulses we have traced, as we watch Spenser at once celebrate his power and face the futility of sustaining, through his power, the life of the poem.

⋐ III ⋑

CONTINENTAL AND ENGLISH

BACKGROUND TO

THE FAERIE QUEENE

One major element in the literary background to *The Faerie Queene* that cannot be treated at any length is the Bible. However, there was no book before his own that Spenser knew better and, while he certainly never presumes to overgo Scripture, he absorbs and involves it at every point in his poem. To understand the English, Protestant literature of the sixteenth and seventeenth centuries, the Bible is the *sine qua non,* particularly (but certainly not only) the various Epistles of the Apostle Paul and the Book of Revelation.

We may, however, remark at more length several major strains of epic poetry, noting poems both before and after *The Faerie Queene.* I am not concerned specifically with sources and influence; Spenser was heavily obliged to some of his predecessors, not at all to many others. In the case of poets who, like Fletcher and Milton, succeeded him, we may be sure Spenser was the influential agent, though this is not the place to trace precise debts. (I have included these poets after Spenser thinking it might be of interest to see where an epic strain went after *The Faerie Queene.*) For critical commentary on the poems mentioned, see the studies noted in the Bibliography, particularly that of T. M. Greene, to which I am indebted throughout this and the preceding section.

I

The first type of Renaissance epic is the poem celebrating national greatness, after Virgil, and using classical deities as characters, after Ovid. Though often Christian in thrust, it is the most obviously classical strain and is the weakest. In this mode, Francis Petrarch wrote his *Africa* (ca. 1338), celebrating Scipio Africanus. He invested all his hopes for immortality in this epic in Latin, but never finished it and is renowned for the Italian love poems he affected to disdain. Angelo Poliziano, or Politian, the most elegant humanist and poet produced by fifteenth-century Florence, began *Le Stanze per la Giostra* (ca. 1475; *Stanzas for the Tourney*) to honor Giuliano, brother of his patron Lorenzo de' Medici. But Giuliano was killed in the Cathedral of Florence during an abortive revolt in 1478, and the poem—incandescent as a Botticelli painting—remains unfinished. Under the patronage of Charles X, the great French poet Pierre Ronsard decided to celebrate France on the Virgilian model. As Aeneas wandered from Troy to Italy to found a royal line, so on the same mission Francus made from Troy to France. The *Franciade* (1572) failed to hold anyone's interest, particularly the poet's; of the projected twenty-four books, only four were completed. The Portuguese poet Luis Camões did finish his ten-book *Os Lusíadas* (1572; translated as *The Lusiad* by Richard Fanshawe in 1655—Lusus, the Trojan who wandered from Troy to Portugal). This strange, splendid poem glorifies the travels of Vasco da Gama and Portugal's mastery of the sea, thoroughly mixes classical and Christian deities, and glows with exotic details which the poet, as widely traveled as da Gama, observed at first hand.

The second type of epic is the poem which is explicitly Christian and often modeled on the Bible or on Biblical episodes. Maffius Vegius, best known for his *Thirteenth Book of the Aeneid* (1427), wrote *Antoniados* (1430), an epic on St. Anthony. The *Parthenicae,* seven poems on the Virgin and various saints, were written between 1481 and 1507 by Battista Spagnuoli, the Carmelite, known as Mantuan after his birthplace, whose Latin pastorals were school texts all over Europe. In *The Reason of Church Government* (1641), Milton considers "epic form" and calls the book of Job "a brief model." The tradition of the "brief epic," as it is called, culminates in *Paradise Regained* (1671) but includes poems like those noted above as well as Jacopo Sannazaro's poem on the birth of Christ, *De Partu Virginis* (1526), the *Christiados* (1535; translated by Cranwell, 1728) of Marco Girolamo Vida, the *Judith* (1574; translated by T. Hudson, 1584) of G. de S. Du Bartas, Giles Fletcher the younger's

Christ's Victorie and Triumph (1610), and G. B. Marino's gory Baroque delicacy, *La Strage dell'Innocenti* (1632; Englished in 1675 by R. T. as *Slaughter of the Innocents*).

A sub-genre of the Christian Biblical poem is the Hexaemeral poem, deriving from early Christian writers, which recounts the seven days of the Creation. Maurice Scève and Torquato Tasso wrote notable poems in this vein, and of course *Paradise Lost* includes the genre, as it includes all others. But the best known Renaissance Hexaemeral poem is Du Bartas' *La Semaine,* made up of *Premier Semaine* (1578) and the unfinished *Second Semaine* (pub. 1584), which was widely read in the influential translation of Joshua Sylvester, *Du Bartas His Divine Weekes and Workes* (1605).

The third strain of Renaissance epic is the most relevant for us because it includes *The Faerie Queene*. This is the Romance epic, or epic of chivalry. Its roots are in the Carolingian *chansons de geste,* the old French epics of war centering on Roland, the Peers, the rebellious vassals, the family of Guillaume d'Orange, and in the Arthurian romances of love, those courtly and sophisticated tales of Lancelot, Guinevere, Tristan, and the rest.

In 1483, Luigi Pulci published his *Morgante,* a long, shrewd burlesque of the solemn Carolingian matter where sarcasm reduces seriousness and grotesques win the hearts of readers. Lord Byron's translation of the first canto is a masterpiece. Written for the household of Lorenzo de' Medici, the *Morgante* takes its name from a slow, simpleminded giant who is only a secondary character but who lingers in the mind as a creature loyal, decent, and humane. In mocking the norms of chivalry and establishing an ironic perspective on his own material, Pulci pushes words, and other recognizable human forms, to their limit. From the level of slang and new linguistic coinages, through his demons, to his giants (Morgante has a slightly smaller friend, Margutte), Pulci roughens the texture of epic and sings a sarcastic hymn to deformity. But he is also very serious, for he is saying we must enjoy life in whatever strange shape it comes, for all is passing. And he tells us what we will hear often again in the Renaissance: a deformed surface may mask Truth, and, if only we can find it, we will be ourselves reformed.

In fifteenth-century Ferrara, mighty Roland fell in love. Matteo Maria Boiardo, erudite soldier and accomplished translator and poet, wrote the *Orlando Innamorato* (1495; *Roland in Love*) and united the Carolingian and Arthurian strains, the worlds of war and love, battlefield and bed. This long, glittering poem, intended to entertain the aristocrats of the Ducal court by limning their deepest fantasies, is a pell-mell tale of swift battle and passionate love. This idealized chronicle of the generous world of knights and lovely ladies was left unfinished, however. Boiardo recognized that the gap between his poem's values and the actualities of the 1480s and 1490s was too great, and art simply gave up before the realities of life.

Precisely the gap between ideal codes of chivalric behavior and actual modes of social behavior, between dreams of knightly nobility and a world where gunpowder blew men and horses into indistinguishable bits is the subject of Ludovico Ariosto's great *Orlando Furioso* (1532; *Roland Mad*. Translated by Sir John Harington, 1591). Intended to complete Boiardo's poem, Ariosto's is an enormous, kaleidoscopic creation on its own, still working the rich vein of traditional stories of love and war but now placing its elegant, shifting surface in ironic juxtaposition to its own grim, savage substance. The poem is an instance of the problem it describes as the poet dares the reader to make the mistake he reads about, the error of assuming appearance is reality. Spenser knew and loved this poem and borrowed from it brilliantly, learning from it a radical truth, that we believe only what we need and want to believe, that no one truly deludes a man but himself. The warnings throughout *The Faerie Queene* to be wary, to be wise, beginning with the first spoken words in the poem when Una warns the Redcross Knight to "Be well aware" (I,i,12), derive ultimately from lessons learned in the bright, deceptive, conservative world of Ariosto.

Spenser knew, and used, two other Italian chivalric epics. He borrowed at times from the long epic of Italy's liberation from the barbarians, *L'Italia Liberata dai Goti* (1547–48) by the humanist Giangiorgio Trissino. This work, written according to Aristotle's rules for narrative, as they were interpreted by the early sixteenth century, and most successful only where it is most derivative, is far inferior to Torquato Tasso's *Gerusalemme Liberata* (1575; pub. 1581. Translated by Edward Fairfax, 1600). Shorter, more consciously contrived than Ariosto's poem, the *Jerusalem Delivered* had to appease the multiple demands of Aristotle's *Poetics*, Counter-Reformation Catholicism, and powerful contemporary literary critics. Tasso unified the chivalric and Christian epic (as, in a different fashion, Spenser would later) by telling of the first Crusade under Godfrey of Bulloigne in 1096 to free the Holy City from the Turks. Doctrinal where Ariosto's was silent or skeptical, moralistic where Ariosto's tended to psychology, beautifully structured where its predecessor seemed free-flowing, Tasso's poem was extremely important for *The Faerie Queene*. Spenser constantly borrowed versions of Nature from Tasso: from Armida's garden (*G.L.* XVI) for Acrasia's Bower of Bliss (*F.Q.* II,xii); from Erminia's pastoral interlude (*G.L.* VII) for Serena's pastoral recuperation (*F.Q.* VI,vi,1–15) and Pastorella's wholesome upbringing (*F.Q.* VI,ix). But even more than Nature, Spenser found in Tasso confirmation for a natural longing. Like Spenser, but in his own fashion, Tasso constantly sought reconciliation and synthesis—of art and nature, city and country, man and woman, mankind and God—and if his efforts to achieve this unity are sometimes desperate, that only reflects the depth of his desire for union and peace. As C. S. Lewis has justly said of Spenser, so also in Tasso the deepest urge is to stop, to sleep, to die—to say, I can no more and here I cease, my armor off, off my horse, no more long way around. In the Jesuit-educated poet of Trentine Italy and the great Protestant poet of Elizabethan England we repeatedly see how profound is the desire to give in and how much it costs to keep going.

In the late sixteenth century—Tasso, Camões, Spenser—the desire to rest both spirit and sense was fundamental. The world was so much with mankind, in religious wars, reformations in doctrine, literature, and politics, in discoveries across the seas and in the skies. Exhilarated and exhausted, the poets of the *fin de siècle*—Tasso, Camões, Spenser—took, at some deep level, exhaustion and the need to sleep as their themes.

II

Spenser learned much from his classical and Continental predecessors in epic. From Virgil, he drew a model of heroic energy, labor, in the service of communal, civic good, and the image of the painful passage of an individual into an institution. From Ovid's *Metamorphoses,* Spenser learned, as all Renaissance poets of Romance epic learned, to make the structure of his poem reflect his sense of life's unceasing mutability. From his immediate Italian predecessors, Spenser took incidents, episodes, motifs, perspectives—the stuff of a vision of man questing for an end to exile in a hostile, shifting, complex world.

From the Italians, however, Spenser drew most obviously. The man who signed his letters to Gabriel Harvey *Immerito* (Unworthy), and whom Harvey addressed as *Signior Immerito,* peoples his poem with characters whose names are drawn from Italian as often as from English, Greek, or Latin. Spenser is the first English poet to divide his poem by the *canto,* like the Italians, and to use the term. Using the octave of the Italian chivalric romance, ABABABCC, Spenser fashions his own, unique stanza: ABABBCBCC, adding a ninth, longer, Alexandrine line. This supple last line echoes back within the stanza and enriches and resolves the complexity of all nine lines while often it provides a link, through rhyme, with the next stanza. Spenser manages to create a stanza that is fuller, more open, and more leisurely as a narrative vehicle than the Italian octave while sacrificing none of the continuity and flow within and between the stanzaic units of the narrative. Spacious, complex, and discrete, the stanza resembles the poem for which it was created— both are sufficient to the complexity and ambiguity of a mutable world where value resides at the center and we live at the edges, which are always blurred.

The Spenserian stanza owes something also (some would say much) to two English stanza forms: English Rhyme Royal, ABABBCC, and the stanza Chaucer uses in *The Monk's Tale,* ABABBCBC. Thus Spenser's stanza is a unique blend of English and foreign elements, as the names in his poem are, as the rarefied, artificial language, used to convey an impression of enchantment and "faery," is a mixture of words Saxon, Anglo-Norman, and Latin in origin. Which is to say the stanza, or the poem, is a typically Renaissance product, fashioned by a poet who used whatever he needed from wherever he found it. It is also to say that the sixteenth century in England was a time for grafting foreign shoots to hardy native stock—one reason why Elizabethan literature can be, by turns, so insular and so universal. We must now turn to the native ground; for, if Spenser respected the classics and admired the Italians, he, like Mulcaster, loved England more. He loved her countryside, her fabulous history, her people; but above all, I think, he loved two things, the English language and the English queen, and we cannot understand the poem that celebrates them unless we look at what he found at home.

III
English Background

On January 11, 1509, at the Sign of the Sun in Fleetstreet, Wynken de Worde published a poem by Stephen Hawes entitled *The Pastime of Pleasure.* The hero, Graunde Amour, meets in a meadow Lady Fame who describes La Belle Pucelle. Enamored, he sets out to find her; at the Tower of Doctrine, he is instructed by Lady Grammar, and then he visits Logic, Rhetoric, Arithmetic, and Music, where La Belle is. They dance, he is shy, Counsel advises they go to the garden. He woos her but she is carried off to foreign lands. Before following, the hero is instructed by Geometry and Astronomy. At the Tower of Chivalry, he is taught by Minerva and knighted. Graunde Amour then meets a dwarf named Godfrey Gobeleive and together they attend a "parliment" with Venus, who sends a letter asking La Belle to be kind. The hero cuts off the three heads of a giant, and Perseverance brings a nice note from La Belle. He defeats a seven-headed giant. Through a dark wooded wilderness, Graunde Amour sees La Belle's palace on an island infested with Privy Malice. Blinded and wounded by this dragon-monster, the hero is saved by a salve administered by his beloved. The monster bursts, they are married. Years of happiness ensue. Then Age arrives, with Policy and Avarice. Death finally takes Graunde Amour away. Lady Fame returns, only to be replaced in this pageant by Time, who claims to rule all. But Time is supplanted by Eternity. After a conventional apology, the poem ends.

Written in Rhyme Royal, this work of nearly 6,000 lines marks a new direction in English poetry. Its author, born perhaps in 1474 or 1475, dead before 1530, educated at Oxford, a youthful groom in the household of Henry VIII, was very much a man of the Middle

Ages. He worshipped John Lydgate, the successor, at least chrono-
logically, of Chaucer. Hawes revered the past. No one today, he
says, writes poetry properly:

> They fayne no fables / pleasaunt and couerte
> But spend theyr tyme / in vaynfull vanyte
> Makynge balades / of feruent amyte
> As gestes and tryfles / without fruytfulnes.
>
> (1389–92)[1]

Yet despite, or perhaps because of, his medieval cast—and what
could be more medieval than a poem tracing the course of true
love by way of the Trivium and Quadrivium—Hawes knows what
kind of poetry should be written. We get a hint in the phrase
"pleasaunt and couerte": Poems should be covert, or allegorical;
dream visions as this one is, or as were William Dunbar's *The
Golden Targe*, Lydgate's *Temple of Glas*, Chaucer's *House of
Fame* and *Parliament of Fowles* or, to go no further back, the
Romance of the Rose. These allegorical dream visions all open
with an Ideal Landscape, a garden or meadow in which the dreamer
either sleeps and dreams or has a vision. From the innumerable
French, English, and Scots poems in this mold, *The Faerie Queene,*
without the mechanical apparatus of vision, draws its dream-like
quality. However, Hawes wants more. He wants poetry not only
couerte, but also *pleasaunt.*

What Hawes means by pleasant is implied when Graunde Amour
arrives at the Castle of Chivalry:

> My name quod I is graunde amoure
> Of late I came fro the toure of doctryne
> Where I attayned all the hygh honoure
> Of the seuen scyences me to enlumyne
> And frome thens I dyde determyne
> Forth to trouaylle to this toure of chyualry
> Where I haue blowen this blast so sodaynly.
>
> (2976–82)

The Porter replies:

> Vnto this toure ye must resorte by ryght
> For to renue that hath be longe decayd
> The floure of chyualry with your hole delyght.
>
> (2984–86)

"With your whole delight". The pleasant poem, of the kind no longer composed, is one that would do what the Porter recommends: Renew the flower of chivalry, that hath been long decayed. Here, finally, is why *The Pastime of Pleasure* is a new departure in English poetry. Hawes wants to combine allegory and chivalry in one poem; he wants in one landscape to contain both the Tower of Doctrine and the Tower of Chivalry. He wants, he says, to write that kind of poem again, though, as C. S. Lewis has pointed out in *The Allegory of Love,* it had never been written before, and would only be truly written later, supremely by Spenser in *The Faerie Queene.*

The general outline of the *Pastime,* an allegory about a man's life, about Love and Death, would have interested Spenser. And indeed many parallels between the two poems have been noted, similarities of language, detail, scene, and episode. Most striking, however, is the fact that Graunde Amour, Youth in *The Example of Virtue,* a shorter version of *The Pastime of Pleasure,* and the Redcross Knight in Book I of *The Faerie Queene,* all wear the same armor of the Christian mentioned by Paul in the Epistle to the Ephesians, 6:13–17:

> Wherefore take unto you the whole armour of God, that ye may be able to withstand in the evil day, and having done all, to stand.
> Stand therefore, having your loins girt about with truth, and having on the breastplate of righteousness;
> And your feet shod with the preparation of the gospel of peace;
> Above all, taking the shield of faith, wherewith ye shall be able to quench all the fiery darts of the wicked.
> And take the helmet of salvation, and the sword of the Spirit, which is the word of God.

We must not assume Spenser took the motif of the Christian armor from Hawes; like Hawes, Spenser took it, as he did so much, from the Bible. But the common borrowing reveals a common preoccupation to combine the themes of chivalry and salvation.

More important than motifs, however, is the tone and feel of Hawes's verse. Hawes is not a great poet; often he is not even a good one. But his language and imagery are worth noting for what they tell us of the early sixteenth century and for what they foreshadow. Graunde Amour first sees Lady Fame:

I sawe come rydynge / in a valaye ferre
A goodly lady / enuyronned aboute
With tongues of fyre / as bryght as ony sterre
That fyry flambles / ensensed alwaye out
Whiche I behelde / and was in grete doubt
Her palfraye swyfte / rennynge as the wynde
With two whyte grehoundes / that were not behynde.

(155–61)

That is quite good: a luminous picture of a lady who is at once very close yet far away, a static, self-contained image of great movement. The frozen, formal vision of horse, lady, and dogs—separate yet together—hardly equals, but is not very unlike, the opening stanza of *The Faerie Queene*.

When the hero first spies La Belle Pucelle, she is with Music:

She [Music] cōmaunded her mynstrelles / ryght anone to play
Mamours the swete / and the gentyll daunce
With la bell pucell / that was fayre and gaye
She me recommaunded / with all pleasaunce
To daunce true mesures / without varyaunce
O lorde god / how glad than was I
So for to daunce / with my swete lady

By her propre hande / soft as ony sylke
With due obeysaunce / I dyde her than take
Her skynne was whyte / as whalles bone or mylke
My thoughtes was rauysshed / I myght not aslake
My brennynge hert / she the fyre dyde make
These daunces truely / musyke hath me tought
To lute or daunce / but it auayled nought

For the fyre kyndled / and waxed more and more
The dauncynge blewe it / with her beaute clere
My hert sekened / and began waxe sore
A mynute .vi. houres / and .vi. houres a yere
I thought it was / so heuy was my chere
But yet for to couer / my grete loue aryght
The outwarde coūtenaunce / I made gladde and lyght.

(1583–1603)

These strangely compelling stanzas tell, with their own clear music, of a young man dancing with a girl he loves and has never seen before. Hawes captures the sense in which you are always approaching the one you love. And who has ever danced with someone he loves and has not been terrified at the delight?

Much in these verses is rude and awkward. Some lines barely scan, others scan not at all. The language is rough, the comparisons conventional—her hand like silk—or homely—her skin white as whalebone or milk. We are finally burdened with the medieval conception of the woman who ennobles (with a hint, in "ravished" thought, of Paul who was taken to the third heaven, II Corinthians, 12:2–4) and the conventional, ultimately Ovidian, language of fire and love and so on. But while Hawes is homely, he is also concrete; while he is halting, he is also communicating—convincing us of something felt; particularly in his hero's struggle to maintain appearances despite his agitation. Perhaps most impressive is the way Hawes's simple music complements the fact that the couple is dancing. Distantly, we hear what we are shown, as the ancient image of music as harmony combines with the sound and movement of the verse to give us, through ear and eye, the youthful, anxious, awkward version of reconciliation.

At the other end of the century, we will hear Theseus say to his Queen:

> We will, fair Queen, up to the mountain's top
> And mark the musical confusion
> Of hounds and echo in conjunction . . .

and she will reply:

> I was with Hercules and Cadmus once . . .
> . . . . Never did I hear
> Such gallant chiding; for, besides the groves,
> The skies, the fountains, every region near
> Seemed all one mutual cry. I never heard
> So musical a discord, such sweet thunder.
> *(Midsummer Night's Dream,* IV,i,120ff)

Here we are with Shakespeare, far from Hawes in every respect, and there is no sense comparing great things and small. But we may note that the same image of harmony and concert is at work, and the same preoccupation with music reconciling opposites is present. And when, in Book VI of *The Faerie Queene,* Calidore hears a "shrill pipe" and thumping feet "That through the woods their eccho did rebound," he investigates:

> There did he see, that pleased much his sight,
> That even he him selfe his eyes envyde,
> An hundred naked maidens lilly white,
> All raunged in a ring, and dauncing in delight;
>
> All they without were raunged in a ring,
> And daunced round; but in the midst of them
> Three other ladies did both daunce and sing,
> The whilest the rest them round about did hemme,
> And like a girland did in compasse stemme:
> And in the middest of those same three was placed
> Another damzell, as a precious gemme
> Amidst a ring most richly well enchaced,
> That with her goodly presence all the rest much graced.
>
> (VI,x,11–12)

Written probably about the same time as Shakespeare's play, 1595 or so, Spenser's passage too makes music as it describes a vision of harmony through dancing and singing. This concert, reconciling nature and art, the creator, Colin Clout, and his creation, is a synthesis on the grandest scale but still uses the old image of music and dance for man and woman in harmony. Colin and the graces —a far cry from Graunde Amour and La Belle Pucelle, all the distance from one whose "skin was white as whalesbone or milk" to "an hundred naked ladies lily white." And yet, while Hawes's homeliness has been polished and refined, still somehow it is the same girl, and that is the point. Not that Hawes was Shakespeare or Spenser, or that Hawes invented the imagery of music, but that from earlier poets like Hawes came ways of seeing and ways of saying; came a sense of the importance of ceremony and a desire to unite opposites. Above all, came a language whose very concreteness, crudity, and awkwardness provided poets like Shakespeare and Spenser not only with material to refine but also with a source of strength, a fertile, native English soil which, if sometimes coarse as soil must be, was also rich.

It is at the level of language we can observe English poets of the Renaissance forging their new worlds, for they all strove to create a language for literature which could compete with the tongues of

Antiquity and the vernaculars of the Continent in majesty, mastery, and power. At the level of language, English poets combined the foreign and the native elements. Often trained in the humanist tradition, with small or large Latin, often with Greek, possessing French and Italian, the Englishman brought to these languages, and all they implied in the way of discipline and tradition, a mother tongue supple and strong, a native language, as it was in Hawes, malleable, emergent, waiting to be finally fashioned. Thus when Spenser does what Hawes wanted to do, reach back and revive the strength of the past, it is Spenser's language that first strikes us. Strange, full of archaism, dialect, "medieval" or "old" English words and forms, a language never spoken anywhere but in Faery Land, it is the result of a Renaissance humanist-poet's conscious attempt to use his native resources and make something new from what was familiar, homely, and old.

When first we meet Florimell, "upon a milkwhite palfrey,"

> Whose face did seeme as cleare as cristall stone,
> And eke through feare as white as whales bone,
>
> (III,i,15)

we remember the girl in Hawes's poem whose skin was "white as whales bone or milk" and we witness the process of constant transformation at the lowest but primary level of language. Here is no question of "influence" or "source," but simply an instance of how earlier poets prepare the verbal ground for cultivation by later ones. From poems like Hawes's *Pastime,* and even more from works now little read but once widely known like Thomas Sackville's *Induction* to *The Mirror for Magistrates* (1563) or George Gascoigne's *Steele Glas* (1576), or the poetry of John Skelton (?1460–?1529), came a rugged vernacular which Spenser could build upon, adapt from, and change. This English, which Spenser knew but did not write, provided his consciously archaized "literary" fabric with strands of basic toughness and native resiliency. Their English gave his a kind of tensile strength. The result is that *The Faerie Queene,* like so many fine "Italianate" cloaks of the day, is made of sturdy English cotswold fleece.

~§ IV ℰ~

MUTABILITY AND HEALTH

It has never been a secret that men die, that the grave awaits us all. The Wheel of Fortune turns, and the highest and lowest are finally the same. The Middle Ages and the Renaissance found this spectacle immensely edifying. "But fortune ys so varyaunte," says Lancelot to Arthur and Gawain, "and the wheele so mutable, that there ys no constaunte abydynge" (*Morte Darthur*, XX,17). It is a very old story, whether we read it in Lydgate's enormous *Fall of Princes* or watch it in the graveyard scene in *Hamlet*.

> If I be rightly enformed of the causes and condition of thy disease, thou languishest with the affection and desire of thy former fortune, and the change of that alone, as thou imaginest, hath overthrowne the state of thy mind. I know the manifold illusions of that monster, exercising most alluring familiarity with them, whome she meaneth to deceive, to the end she may confounde them with intolerable griefe, by forsaking them upon the sudden, whose nature, customes and desert, if thou remembrest, thou shalt know, that thou neither diddest possesse, nor hast lost anything of estimation in it; . . . [Fortune] hath kept that constancie in thy affaires, which is proper to her, in being mutable. (Book II, prose I)

So Lady Philosophy to Boethius in the *Consolation of Philosophy*.[1] This work, composed ca. A.D. 524, in prose and verse, is a dream vision and recommends in the face of adversity a stoical self-sufficiency and faith in God. Here Philosophy advises we ignore Fortune. But there is a note we cannot ignore, the fundamental paradox that would haunt Spenser, that the only thing constant is change.

> If thus the world never long tarie,
> The same, but often varie:
> On fading fortunes then relie,

41

> Trust to those goods that flie.
> An everlasting law is made,
> That all things borne shall fade.
>   (Book II, verse II)

"Nothing is sure that growes on earthly grownd," says Spenser (*F.Q.* I,ix,11), and the ancient preoccupation with mutability spreads into every part of *The Faerie Queene,* becoming more insistent at the end.

> But what on earth can alwayes happie stand?
>   (V,iii,9)

> All flesh is frayle, and full of ficklenesse,
> Subject to fortunes chance, still chaunging new;
> What haps to day to me tomorrow may to you.
>   (VI,i,41)

> Such is the weakenesse of all mortall hope;
> So tickle is the state of earthly things,
> That ere they come unto their aymed scope,
> They fall too short of our fraile reckonings,
> And bring us bale and bitter sorrowings,
> In stead of comfort, which we should embrace:
> This is the state of keasars and of kings.
> Let none therefore, that is in meaner place,
> Too greatly grieve at any his unlucky case.
>   (VI,iii,5)

By listening one last time to Hawes, we may hear the way Spenser heard things before he made his own music, and better understand how the old commonplaces about mutability and fortune could assume such central importance in Spenser's epic poem.

Graunde Amour and La Belle Pucelle live many years in "Ioye" and then one day an old man comes to the hero's room: "Obey he sayd I must you nedes a reste / My name is age" (5354–55). Graunde Amour continues to think he has many days left him when suddenly he dies. Remembrance places a long epitaph on his grave which ends:

> O mortall folke / you may beholde and se
> How I lye here / somtyme a myghty knyght
> The ende of Ioye / and all prospertye

Is dethe at last / through his course and myght
After the day there cometh the derke nyght
For though the day be neuer so longe
At last the belles ryngeth to euensonge.

(5474–80)

Lady Fame prepares to make his name immortal, but Time scolds
her for presumption. For, he says, does not he destroy every earthly
thing? And then, recalling the role of the city in epic and in Spenser,
we see it all:

In tyme Troye the cyte was edefyed
By tyme also was the dystruccyon
Nothynge without tyme can be fortefyed
No erthely Ioye nor trybulacyon
Without tyme is for to suffre passyon
The tyme of erthe was our dystruccyon
And the tyme of erthe was our redempcyon.

(5691–97)

"Edefyed—dystruccyon;" "Dystruccyon—redempcyon." The fram-
ing words of the stanza catch the double impulse within epic, of
creation and decay; the city of man passing, the city of God coming
—while like sledgehammer blows, we hear "tyme," "tyme," "the
tyme of erthe," "the tyme of erthe." Perhaps Spenser's eye was caught
here. What was true for Troy would be true for Troynovant.[2]

But, says Time, he too must pass: "And after me is dame eternyte"
(5746). She now proclaims her power:

O mortall folke reuolue in your mynde
That worldly Ioye and frayle prospertye
What is it lyke but a blaste of wynde
For you therof can haue no certaynte
It is now so full / of mutabylyte
Set not your mynde vpon worldly welthe
But euermore regarde your soules helthe.

(5775–81)

"For you thereof can haue no certaynte / It is now so full, of mutabylyte." This gloomy, rhyming moralism, old as Ecclesiastes, always implying the loss of a better time, runs like an ordering chord
through The Pastime. Back where we began, at the discussion of
poetry, Hawes urged us to attend to Master Lydgate's poetry:

A good ensample / for vs to dyspyse
This worlde so full / of mutabylyte
In whiche no man / can haue a certaynte.

(1349–51)

The irony in the rhyming harmony of those opposites, mutability and certainty, is one Spenser would have enjoyed, and it is a rhyme he himself adapts. The couplet with same rhyme but one different word occurs in the middle of the last stanza of *The Faerie Queene,* as the poet muses on Nature's assertion that she rules the heavens, Mutability the earth:

Then gin I thinke on that which Nature sayd,
Of that same time when no more change shall be;
But stedfast rest of all things, firmely stayd
Upon the pillours of eternity,
That is contrayr to Mutabilitie:
For all that moveth doth in change delight:
But thence-forth all shal rest eternally
With Him that is the god of Sabbaoth hight:
O that great Sabbaoth God graunt me that Sabaoths sight.

(VII,viii,2)[3]

This is the great cry of all Romance literature, the yearning for Revelation in the midst of flux. Spenser gazes back at his vast, complex, and changing fiction and longs for a vision (sight) and a locus (site) of permanence. He yearns for no more fiction but stable and abiding truth. The poet craves what all the inhabitants of Faery Land have sought and none ever finds. Only exile, life at the edges, is permanent. Until we die.

What we see Spenser sharing with Hawes but developing further is a deep sense of disease, of gnawing unrest and corrosive decay, and a common desire to write a poem despite and because of it. Where Spenser surpasses his earlier English predecessors is in his knowledge that the forces of mutability are not only fatal to the city without, to the public man, but also to the mansion within, the private world. Spenser knows these two realms are mutually dependent because he has learned the lessons of Humanism.

Humanism was essentially a program of radical ethical education, based on the Greek and Roman classics, devised by those who had found in the political and moral values of the ancients (particularly the Romans) precepts that furthered the civilized life of man in the secular sphere. Humanism informed the Renaissance with a keen awareness of the mutual needs of the private and the public worlds, and of the final reliance of the public dimension of rational, civic action upon the private, properly fashioned impulses of the individual mind. All the mythology of the Renaissance, including the myth that was Neo-Platonism, and much of Renaissance literature, strove to forge the links between the private and public worlds of man, and thus provide for the Many the perceptions and ethical wisdom of the One.

So where the Middle Ages displayed hoary commonplaces about the mutability of man and of cities, the Renaissance insisted that the connection between them be made, that we see how a city falls because men have first decayed within. Like the Middle Ages, the Renaissance believed in the didactic role and curative powers of literature, the restorative potency of words which were, after all, but versions of the Word. But the Renaissance, always absorbing this medieval knowledge, knew that if literature could purge and make wholesome and sound (in Spenser's words) the body politic, literature must remind us that first and always the individual soul was at stake. When at I,vii,7, Redcross is "Both carelesse of his health, and of his fame," we know he is disregarding his private and his public realms, his inner well-being and his social effectiveness. The order is important in establishing how, for a while, Redcross loses his claims and rights of citizenship and sinks slowly towards Despair.

Spenser's larger concerns with mutability spring from his concerns for the specific demands of what Hawes called the "soules health." In perilous curiosity about the Cave of Despair, a crucial episode in the poem, Redcross asks:

> 'How may a man,' said he, 'with idle speach
> Be wonne to spoyle the castle of his health?'
> (I,ix,31)

In Book VI, Sir Calepine so assiduously tends Serena

> That the faint sprite he did revoke againe
> To her fraile mansion of mortality.
> (VI,iii,28)

Spenser always thinks of the human spirit as a city within, and sees it as a frail edifice, constantly in need of defense. Of course, the imagery of the spiritual edifice was not new with Spenser. Sir Thomas Elyot had written a book in 1539 called *The Castel of Helth* because, as he says, he was "studiouse about the weale of his country"—a good Humanist attitude and phrase. In his *Induction*, Sackville had compared himself to

> him that with the feruent feuer stryves
> When sicknees seekes his castell health to skale.
>
> (129–30)

The "soules health" was even more a constant concern in literature. The great English printer William Caxton sees literature itself as the primary defender of our spiritual well-being. In his epilogue to his edition of the *Consolation of Philosophy* (1478), Caxton says he prints the book "In hopying that it shal prouffite moche peple to the wele helth of their soules;" and in the "prohemye" to his second edition of *The Canterbury Tales* (1484), he urges us to read the tales and profit "Vnto the helthe of our sowles." [4] Indeed, the phrase itself occurs in Chaucer, when the Parson exhorts his congregation not to confess for base motives "but oonly for the doute of Jhesu Crist and the heele of thy soule" (*Parson's Tale*, 1023).[5]

Spenser's fundamental concerns, deepened by his humanistic perspective, are old ones. It is fitting that those concerns also belong to Chaucer's Parson, for Chaucer was Spenser's great master. Though it may seem overmuch the long way around, one way to the core of *The Faerie Queene* is through the poet of *The Canterbury Tales*.

⊷ V ⊶

CHAUCER AND SPENSER

In Book IV, Spenser commences the story of Cambel and Triamond by referring to what "antique storys tellen us":

> Though now their acts be no where to be found,
> As that renowmed poet them compyled
> With warlike numbers and heroicke sound,
> Dan Chaucer, well of English undefyled,
> On Fames eternall beadroll worthie to be fyled.
>
> (IV,ii,32)

Spenser then "completes" the unfinished *Squire's Tale* of Chaucer, partly by borrowing from *The Knight's Tale* as well. (Thus offering, incidentally, another instance of one epic poet's desire to "overgo" an earlier great master of narrative.) But Spenser is acknowledging here a greater debt than simply the origins of a story. In more profound ways, Chaucer is Spenser's source; Chaucer is the "pure well head of poesie" (VII,vii,9) from which Spenser drew poetic strength all his life.

In the "June" eclogue of *The Shepheardes Calender,* Spenser, or Colin Clout, laments that

> The god of shepheards, Tityrus, is dead,
> Who taught me, homely as I can, to make.
>
> (81–82)

and in "December" we learn that Colin "of Tityrus his songs did lere" (4). Tityrus is Chaucer, and here Spenser pays his English master the highest tribute, for Tityrus had been Virgil's name for himself in his *Eclogues*—as the reference to "the Romish Tityrus" and his three great poems makes clear ("October," 55–60). In Renaissance fashion, the medieval poet is honored through the classical allusion.

Many were the means by which a young Elizabethan poet could come under the tutelage of Chaucer. From Caxton's first two editions of *The Canterbury Tales* (1478; 1484) through the collected works in the editions of Pynson (1526), Thynne (1532; 1542; 1546; 1555), Stow (1561), and Speght (1598), Chaucer was represented at Elizabeth's death in nearly a dozen reprints and pirated editions, each increasingly marred by errors and freighted with apocrypha. Yet despite the corrupt texts and sixteenth-century ignorance that Chaucer pronounced his final *e,* Spenser's indebtedness to Chaucer was deep and genuine. In addition to specific borrowings, like the *Squire's Tale,* Spenser undoubtedly learned much in general from Chaucer's allegories and visions—*The Book of the Duchess, The House of Fame, The Parliament of Fowles,* the *Prologue to the Legend of Good Women.* Even more importantly, Spenser could find in Chaucer brilliant crystallizations of Romance themes and folktale motifs in forms that must have confirmed and encouraged his own plans.

For instance, in the opening lines of *The Wife of Bath's Tale,* we are in the land of Faery.

> In th' olde dayes of the Kyng Arthour,
> Of which that Britons speken greet honour,
> Al was this land fulfild of fayerye.
> The elf-queene, with hir joly compaignye,
> Daunced ful ofte in many a grene mede.
>
> (857–61)

And when the young hero of this tale rode "under a forest syde" and

> saugh upon a daunce go
> Of ladyes foure and twenty, and yet mo;
> Toward the whiche daunce he drow ful yerne,
> In hope that som wysdom sholde he lerne.
> But certeinly, er he cam fully there,
> Vanysshed was this daunce, he nyste where,
>
> (991–96)

we are inevitably reminded of Calidore's vision of the dancing maidens on Mount Acidale:

Therefore resolving, what it was, to know,
Out of the wood he rose, and toward them did go.

But soone as he appeared to their vew,
They vanisht all away out of his sight,
And cleane were gone, which way he never knew.
(VI,x,17–18)

In both passages, we have images of harmony in Nature through a dance; in both, the knight's desire for further knowledge destroys the vision, and he is left with a single figure—an old hag in Chaucer, a shepherd-poet in Spenser. Indeed, the similarities of language suggest Spenser may have had the specific Chaucerian passage in mind. But direct influence is not the question; the motif of "otherworldly ladies" is a staple of medieval romance. What Chaucer distills, and Spenser treats here and everywhere in his poem, is the evanescence of vision, the frailty of harmony, the vulnerability of ideal revelations to the pressures of the world. In both passages, the hero's movement from the wood (the human condition) to the green full of harmony (human hope) results in disappointment when the vision vanishes. The impulse to go from the wild edges to what one hopes is the ordered clearing at the center—of the world, of the self—is the great movement of *The Faerie Queene*. And the desire to know and to possess in the flesh of the mind the ideal vision is Spenser's great theme.

In his *Tale of Sir Thopas*, Chaucer also deals with this movement and this theme. *Sir Thopas*, a brief, incomplete parody of a kind of traditional romance, would have initially struck a self-conscious Renaissance poet because the tale is told by the pilgrim named Chaucer, a character reticent, portly, with something—the Host says—"elvyssh" in his face. In this tale, the ubiquitous motifs of Celtic folklore—forest nap, otherworldly lady, unseen beloved—are managed in a burlesque manner which at once crystallizes and capsizes the values of Romance fiction.

Sir Thopas "priketh thurgh a fair forest" (754), and this verb for spurring a horse is emphasized throughout Chaucer's tale as Sir Thopas circles around and around. Finally interrupted by the exasperated Host, the pilgrim breaks off the tale at the words "Til on a day," words that echo the opening line of the adventure, "And so bifel upon a day." The teller of the tale is a type of Sir Thopas and the structure of his tale imitates the circularity of Sir Thopas' roundabout adventures, life at the edges.

At the center, however, is the vision Thopas had when asleep in the wood:

> Me dremed al thys nyght, pardee,
> An elf-queene shal my lemman be
> And slepe under my goore.
> An elf-queene wol I love, ywis,
> For in this worlde no womman is
> Worthy to be my make
> In towne;
> Alle othere wommen I forsake,
> And to an elf-queene I me take
> By dale and eek by downe!
>
> (787–96)

In search of his elf-queen, Sir Thopas comes to "The contree of Fairye / So wilde" (802–3) and meets a giant who tells him:

> Herre is the queene of Fayerye,
> With harpe and pipe and symphonye,
> Dwellynge in this place.
>
> (814–16)

But he never finds her.

The focus of Thopas' experience is the Faery Queene, whose person he seeks after a vision in a wood. Precisely the situation of Spenser's Prince Arthur, who confesses to Una that once he slept in a forest and

> by my side a royall mayd
> Her daintie limbes full softly down did lay:
> So fayre a creature yet saw never sunny day.
>
> Most goodly glee and lovely blandishment
> She to me made, and badd me love her deare;
> For dearly sure her love was to me bent,
> As, when just time expired, should appeare.
> But whether dreames delude, or true it were,
> Was never hart so ravisht with delight,
> Ne living man like wordes did ever heare,

As she to me delivered all that night;
And at her parting said, she Queene of Faries hight.

When I awoke, and found her place devoyd,
And nought but pressed gras where she had lyen,
I sorrowed all so much as erst I joyd,
And washed all her place with watry eyen.
From that day forth I lov'd that face divyne:
From that day forth I cast in carefull mynd,
To seeke her out with labor and long tyne,
And never vow to rest, till her I fynd:
Nyne monethes I seek in vain, yet ni'll that vow unbynd.

(I,ix,13–15)

Arthur's quest is not completed in the poem, but his account of his search to make human the divine face of his beloved is a good description in brief of the movement of the whole *Faerie Queene*. This revelation is the center of value in Spenser's poem. Each knight's quest is a version of Arthur's; each knight is a part of him, as they all seek their ideal in the world and all ride in from the edges, hoping to be reconciled finally in that great central clearing in the woods, the court of Gloriana, where vision will be flesh.

Chaucer's Sir Thopas and Spenser's Prince Arthur are closely related. They represent opposite views of the same drive in from the periphery of existence to experience's visionary core. But what was burlesque in Chaucer is very serious in Spenser. And because Spenser is the solemn adaptor of Chaucer's ironic tale, it has become obligatory, particularly among students of Chaucer, to assert that Spenser has no sense of humor, no notion of burlesque and fun.

We may make two observations. First, it is perfectly true Spenser does not have Chaucer's humor, but no one else does either. Chaucer is unique and glorious. It is not true, however, to say Spenser has no taste, or gift, for burlesque or irony. All the episodes in *The Faerie Queene* that involve Braggadocchio, Trompart, and the False Florimell, for instance, are precisely burlesques on chivalric behavior, that is, on the behavior of everyone else in the poem. Not burlesque in the deft, shrewd, incomparable manner of Chaucer, but it is finally nonsense to tax one great poet because he is not like another.

Second, we may observe of *The Tale of Sir Thopas* that while it is burlesque, it is not *in toto* a joke. Chaucer was not the first, or last, poet to deal humorously with a serious theme, and if Spenser borrowed from Chaucer's matter while ignoring his manner, we need not necessarily conclude that Spenser was ignorant, deaf, or humorless. We may rather assume Spenser found in Chaucer a motif sufficiently formulated to allow him to adapt the essence without the form. Renaissance writers, as we have seen, are programmatically eclectic. Neither Ariosto nor Shakespeare, Spenser, Rabelais nor Cervantes worries about where his material comes from; he is only concerned to adapt what he needs from what the world offers.

Chaucer provided Spenser, however, with more than simply motifs and formulations of themes, important as these are. As we saw in our discussion of the Spenserian stanza, Spenser also learned from Chaucer's rhymes and, even more, from his meters and his rich and resonant language. Spenser learned finally from Chaucer's "style" in its largest sense; he found first in Chaucer what he would find later in himself, that least glamorous but most distinguishing trait of only the greatest poets, a basic balance, a radical common-sense and sanity. It is not too much to say, I think, that Chaucer was to Spenser what Virgil was to Dante—the poet who showed him the way.

Chaucer was the great native influence on Spenser from beyond his own time. Yet there was another one too, a figure we have already identified as central to *The Faerie Queene,* and that is Arthur. Arthur the Prince binds the poem together much as Arthur the King, through legend and fable, bound for centuries the people of England. To appreciate his role in the poem, we must appreciate Arthur's massive and mythic role in the life of the English.

❧ VI ☙

ARTHUR:

HISTORY AND MYTH

When we think of Spenser's part in the Elizabethan revival of chivalry, we ought not assume that only poems like Hawes's *Pastime* or the Italian romances provided the renovative literary impulse. There was also Sir Thomas Malory's *Morte Darthur,* first printed by Caxton in 1485 and then reprinted four more times within a century.

Malory, who died in 1471, was in prison for much of the last twenty years of his life and presumably wrote his book there. In his preface, Caxton reveals how Malory may have spent his last years when the printer says he was urged

> to enprynte a book of the noble hystoryes of the sayd king Arthur /
> and of certeyn of his knyghtes after a copye vnto me delyuerd / whyche
> copye Syr Thomas Malorye dyd take oute of certayn bookes of frensshe
> and reduced it in to Englysshe. (*Caxton,* ed. Crotch, p. 94)

What Malory reduced, or translated, into his swift, vigorous, simple, and often moving English prose were various French poems and prose works, descended from earlier thirteenth-century French prose narratives, about Arthur, his knights, and their adventures. He also drew on two fourteenth-century English poems, an alliterative one (*Morte Arthure*) and a stanzaic one (*Le Morte Arthur*).

Even more interesting than the occasion is Caxton's reason for printing the book:

> to the entente that noble men may see and lerne the noble actes of
> chyualrye / *the Jentyl and vertuous dedes that some knyghtes vsed in
> tho dayes* / by whyche they came to honour / and how they that were
> vycious were punysshed and ofte put to shame and rebuke . . . (*Cax-
> ton,* ed. Crotch, 94)

Here let us set part of another preface:

> The generall end therefore of all the booke is *to fashion a gentleman or noble person in vertuous and gentle discipline:* which for that . . . I chose the historye of King Arthure, as most fitte for the excellency of his person, being made famous by many mens former workes, and also furthest from the daungers of envy, and suspition of present time.

So wrote Spenser in the *Letter to Ralegh* prefacing *The Faerie Queene.* I have italicized the common element in each passage, the didactic desire to renew chivalric virtues on the model of Arthur. The "Jentyl and vertuous dedes" that Caxton wants to display are emblems of the "vertuous or gentle discipline" Spenser hopes to inculcate in his readers. From Caxton, Spenser did not necessarily take these specific words or any others. But he did take the example and figure of Caxton's "most renomed crysten Kyng" Arthur. Spenser found the great English king in a great English book.

At the end of Book II, canto ix, of *The Faerie Queene,* Prince Arthur and Guyon find "antique registers" in the library of Eumnestes at the top of Alma's Castle. Arthur picks up

> An auncient booke, hight *Briton Moniments,*
> That of this lands first conquest did devize,
> And old divisions into regiments,
> Till it reduced was to one mans governments.
> (59)

and Guyon reads *"Antiquitee of Faery Lond,"* where

> Th' ofspring of Elves and Faryes there he fond,
> As it delivered was from hond to hond.
> (60)

Arthur reads history, Guyon fiction; Arthur looks into chronicle, Guyon into myth. These two types of narrative are fused in *The Faerie Queene,* a poem very like the "antique rolles" (I, proem 2) the poet requests of Clio, muse of History (or is it Calliope, muse of Epic?). *The Faerie Queene* is history and myth, the fabulous truth about England, a book similar to those "old records from auncient times derivd" (II,ix,57) which adorn the walls of Eumnestes' study.

Guyon's book is described at II,x,70–81, a great

> And ample volume, that doth far excead
> My leasure, so long leaves here to repeat.
> (70)

There were such books around; one was the English version by Sir John Bourchier, Lord Berners, of *Huon of Bordeaux,* printed by Wynken de Worde about 1534, which introduced Oberon, King of Fairies, to England. But whatever Guyon's book, it is long, fabulous, full of the otherworldly truth about this world, a book fit for this knight of Gloriana and very like the one he is in. Arthur's volume celebrates England's green and pleasant land and chronicles her development from vile and brutish origins to where

> After him Uther, which Pendragon hight,
> Succeeding—There abruptly it did end,
> Without full point, or other cesure right.
> (II,x,68)

Arthur's reading offers an account up to him, or up to King Arthur. This book is described before and at much greater length than Guyon's; it sets forth the solid ground on which the Knights of Maidenhead walk, terrain which at their tread becomes (in Bishop Hurd's phrase) "enchanted ground."

From our point of view, however, the "historical" origins of England are themselves fabulous—solid "facts" veined with fiction. History writing in the modern sense was only just developing with the Italian Humanists and historians, and it would be several generations before English historical writing absorbed all the new lessons about discovering and weighing sources and before Englishmen appropriated the sense of temporal distance we recognize as a necessity for the writing of history.

As Erwin Panofsky remarks, the emergence of historical perspective is connected with the development of other Renaissance ideas of perspective. By looking at the origins and development of the story of King Arthur, who was made famous "in many mens former workes" as Spenser says to Ralegh, we will see how Spenser distinguished history from myth in his own day, and how he made myth of history in his epic poem.[1]

I

To gain our perspective on the story of Arthur, we may begin with a writer who had achieved, through long study, his own perspective on the past. Near the end of Book III of his *History of Britain* (begun in 1640; pub. 1670), Milton says he thinks his own day, "more than any since the first fabulous times, to be surcharg'd with all the idle fancies of posterity." And when he immediately proceeds to discuss Arthur, he expresses dismay at the traditional accounts:

> But who *Arthur* was, and whether ever any such reign'd in *Britain*, hath bin doubted heertofore, and may again with good reason. For the Monk of *Malmsbury*, and others whose credit hath sway'd most with the learneder sort, we may well perceave to have known no more of this *Arthur* 500 years past, nor of his doeings, then we now living; And what they had to say, transcrib'd out of *Nennius*, a very trivial writer yet extant, which hath already bin related. Or out of a *British* Book, the same which he of *Monmouth* set forth, utterly unknown to the World, till more than 600 years after the dayes of *Arthur* . . .
> (Columbia Edition, *Works* X, 127–28)

Here is historical perspective, the awareness of distance between the perceiver and the events, and between the events themselves. Milton's skepticism, by no means original with him, is impressive because of its scale.[2] And if we note that Milton, in weighing his sources, manages to tell the fabulous facts about Arthur while denying their historical validity, nevertheless this is an improvement over most earlier writers who were content to accept the Arthurian legend as it had come down from the Middle Ages.

Milton knew the proper sources for the myth of Arthur. Nennius, author of a *Historia Brittonum* (ca. 800) makes the first extant written reference to Arthur, and says he was a "dux bellorum"— not a king but a leader in war, who led the Britons to victory in twelve battles over the pagans. In chronicles and accounts of miracles from the tenth to the thirteenth centuries, we find Arthur referred to as King, but "he of *Monmouth*" makes the most lasting contribution. A Welsh-born canon at Oxford, Geoffrey of Monmouth (ca. 1100–ca. 1152) composed the *Historia Regum Britannia* (printed at Paris, 1509; 1517) and told the life of Arthur from Book VIII, chapter 19, to Book IX, chapter 2. Geoffrey says he drew on an ancient book in the British tongue (which would be Welsh or Breton), but Milton's skepticism concerning this claim is shared by subsequent historians as well. In addition to traditional accounts, Geoffrey drew on his imagination, and his recital is ultimately the source for all other accounts of Arthur.

The material passed from Geoffrey's Latin prose to vernacular tongues, particularly to the Norman Wace (ca. 1100–1175), in whose *Roman de Brut* occurs the first written reference to the Round Table. Using Bede, Geoffrey, and Wace, a Worcestershire priest named Layamon wrote his *Brut* (completed ca. 1205). Ten thousand lines, or one-third of the poem, are devoted to Arthur, and the role of the Round Table is much expanded. The first in English, Layamon's account informs in some way all later English works in poetry and prose on Arthur, Merlin, Gawain, Tristan, Lancelot, and Perceval.

By now the myth of Arthur is part of the chronicles, those "historical" works that simply repeated the fictions and facts imbedded in previous compilations. We find Arthur in Ralph Higden's enormous *Polychronicon* and in the *Chronicle* of John Hardyng, who draws not only on Geoffrey and Layamon but also on the growing number of poems glorifying Arthur and his knights.[3]

Skepticism concerning the stories of Arthur appears in Robert Faybyn's *New Chronicles of England and France*, published in 1516, though mixed with the skepticism is a native pride in the person and deeds of Arthur.[4] This peculiar mixture would appear for succeeding generations, with stress now on one element in the mix, now on another, and some of this old attitude still seems to cling, despite his lofty vantage point, to Milton's account of Arthur. The most concerted assault, however, on the historical validity of the Arthurian matter and origins of Britain was made by an Italian humanist. At the request of Henry VII, Polydore Vergil wrote a history of England in sixteen books which was finally printed at Basel in 1534. Geoffrey's long recital was now criticized according to the principles of the new historiography. Because he was an Italian attacking the most cherished British hero, Polydore and his book became anathema to succeeding squadrons of patriotic English antiquarians. Nothing circulates a rumor faster than its denial, and the mighty warrior King was now insulated by doughty defenders.

John Leland wrote a tract defending (and even praising) Geoffrey's Arthurian lore and then in 1544 he published in Latin a work translated later by Richard Robinson as *A Learned and True Assertion of the original Life, Actes, and death of the most Noble, Valiant, and Renouned Prince Arthur, King of Greate Britain* (1582). Defending Arthur in Latin is like jousting with bicycles— some of the original spirit is lost—but Leland's treatise was followed by others in 1542, 1548, and 1550, each as "learned" and rabidly patriotic as the last.

Much more was at issue here than simply the convictions of loyal antiquarians versus the methodology of foreign humanists. Politics was at issue. The Tudor family had long since recognized and appreciated the political benefits to be reaped from a lively, or revived, interest in the Welsh Arthur. Henry VII made much of his descent from the Welsh Owen Tudor, and at his coronation in 1485 had displayed a banner with the Red Dragon of Cadwalader on it. By also claiming descent from Brutus, the Trojan, Henry was able cunningly to incarnate the Trojan and Arthurian myths of Britain in his royal person. The King carefully burnished his Arthurian aura. When a son was born to him on September 19, 1486, Henry named him Arthur and later made him the first Prince of Wales. The boy's death in April of 1502 deprived England of another King Arthur and a younger son was installed as Prince of Wales. After this son became Henry VIII, he annexed Wales to England.

Here Tudor policy produces what it wants—Arthurian property. The Royal claim to Arthurian descent furthered its claim to the empire of its ancestor. The roots of the Tudor line became a matter of popular public record; Elizabeth, great-great granddaughter of Owen Tudor, could be celebrated in 1587 by Thomas Churchyard as

> she that sits in reagall Throne,
> With Scepter, Sword, and Crowne.
> (Who came from *Arthurs* rase and lyne).[5]

The Queen buttressed her claims to Scotland and Ireland with her descent from Cadwalader and Arthur. The once and future King might never return but the Tudors hoped his kingdom would.[6] This resurgence of Arthurian interest, nourished by Royal policy and antiquarian patriotism, was part of what A. L. Rowse calls England's exploration of herself, part of her growing awareness of who she was through a probing of what she had been. The revival of Arthur, all of a piece with the Elizabethan love of chivalry, pomp, and pageantry, was not however confined to the aristocratic and learned. There was, for instance, the club that Richard Robinson, ubiquitous hack, described in his booklet *The Ancient Order, Societié and Vnitie Laudable of Prince Arthur and his knightly Armorie of the Round Table; with a Threefold Assertion, friendly in favour and furtherance of English Archery at this day* (1583). Composed of fifty-eight members, each with an Arthurian name, this group existed to promote archery, fellowship, and the good old days—a Rotary Club with bows and arrows. Justice Shallow, as he tells Falstaff, was once a member:

> I remember at Mile End Green, when I lay at Clement's Inn—I was then Sir Dragonet in Arthur's show.
>
> (*2 Henry IV*, III,ii,298–300)

Another, more substantial member was Richard Mulcaster, Spenser's formidable and patriotic teacher at Merchant Taylors' School.

The Arthurian stories and myth also lived in the streets and the theaters. There must have been numerous ballads similar to the one entered by Richard Jones in the Stationer's Register in 1566 called "*a pleasaunte history of an adventurus knyghte of kyng ARTHUR's Courte.*" We know there were plays. Thomas Hughes' *The Misfortunes of Arthur* (1588) survives, and several others on similar themes, now lost, are noted in Henslowe's Diary for the Springs of 1597 and 1598.

Not everyone, however, was enthusiastic about Arthurian poems, histories, and ballads. Roger Ascham inveighed against the old days when certain books were widely read:

> one for example, *Morte Arthure*; the whole pleasure of which books standeth in two speciall poyntes, in open mans slaughter and bold bawdrye—[7]

though, corrupting as it was, ten *Morte Arthures* were not one tenth as harmful as "those bookes made in *Italie* and translated in England" (*The Scholemaster*, 1570). Nothing was more satisfying to numerous Elizabethans than an anti-Catholic sally, and here Malory's old book is condemned for the Old Religion, though patriotism forbade placing anything English on the lowest level of some things Italian. Later Thomas Nashe fulminated, as only he could, against

> those worne out impressions of the feyned no where acts of Arthur of the rounde table, Arthur of litle Brittaine, Sir Tristram, Hewon of Burdeaux, the Squire of low degree, the foure sons of Amon, with in-finite others. (*The Anatomie of Absurditie*, 1589)

In *Palladis Tamia* (1598), Francis Meres condemns, as "no lesse hurtfull to youth than the workes of Machiavell to age," not only *"Arthur of the Round Table"* but twenty-two other titles as well. As the allusion to Machiavelli makes clear, the poems, romances, and ballads on Arthurian themes were viewed as subversive of decent morals and the public good. The Arthurian fictions, in this view, were not the wholesome literature many had, and many still, thought they were. There are traces here of Plato's objections to poets in his *Republic*, Book IX, and this attitude, magnified by the fanatic moralism of the Puritans, would succeed in closing the theaters of London in 1642.

Spenser, as we will see, shares this distrust of poetry in his own special way; but he also shares more fully in the view of his literary contemporaries who named the old matter, and all of literature, with respect and affection. In his *Apology for Poetry* (composed ca. 1583, pub. 1595), Sir Philip Sidney said poetry is the companion of the camps, learning is friend to arms: "I dare undertake, *Orlando Furioso*, or honest King *Arthur*, will never displease a Souldier." George Puttenham confessed he had written a "brief *Romance* or historicall ditty in the English tong, of the Isle of great *Britaine*" should the company be

> desirous to heare of old adventures & valiaunces of noble knights in times past, as are those of King *Arthur* and his knights of the round table, Sir *Bevys of Southampton*, *Guy of Warwicke*, and others like. (*The Arte of English Poesie*, 1589)

Nor did the light of Arthur dim in the next century. William Drummond of Hawthornden records that Ben Jonson told him: "For a Heroik poeme . . . ther was no such ground as King Arthur's fiction" (1619). And such an epic song on Arthur was promised in *Mansus* (ll. 78–84) and *Epitaphium Damonis* (ll. 161–72) by the young Milton, though the Arthurian matter that was so promising in 1639 and 1640 was omitted from the epic materials displayed in *The Reason of Church Government* (1641). John Dryden actually wrote an opera entitled *King Arthur* (1691) and referred to Arthur as an epic subject in *"The Original and Progress of Satire"* two years later. Unfortunately, the only sustained poetic attempts were those by Sir Richard Blackmore, *Prince Arthur* (1695) and *King Arthur* (1697). While all good things must come to an end, the poems of Blackmore are not the miraculous boat to Avalon we might have hoped for.

II

In 1587, when the Arthurian revival was at its peak, Maurice Kyffin sounded a clarion call:

> Ye Bryttish Poets, *Repeat in Royall Song,*
> (*VVith waightie woords, vsde in King* Arthurs *daies*)
> Th' Imperial Stock, *from whence your* Queene *hath sprong;*
> *Enstall in verse your* Princesse *lasting prayes:*
> Percerddiaid, *play on Aunciente Harp, and Crowde:*
> Atceiniaid, *sing her prayses pearcing lowd.*
> (*The Blessednes of Brytaine*)[8]

His challenge did not go unheeded. Spenser puts both Arthur and Elizabeth at the core of *The Faerie Queene.*

So much more profitable and gratious is doctrine by ensample, then by rule. So have I laboured to doe in the person of Arthure: whome I conceive, after his long education by Timon, to whom he was by Merlin delivered to be brought up, so soone as he was borne of the Lady Igrayne, to have seen in a dream or vision the Faery Queen, with whose excellent beauty ravished, he awaking resolved to seeke her out, and so being by Merlin armed, and by Timon thoroughly instructed, he went to seeke her forth in Faerye Land. In that Faery Queene I meane glory in my generall intention, but in my particular

I conceive the most excellent and glorious person of our soveraine the
Queene, and her kingdom in Faery Land. (*Letter to Ralegh*)

As we said at the outset of this chapter, *The Faerie Queene* contains both fable and history, myth and actuality, and Arthur, who
appears in all six completed books, is the prism through which the
two perspectives on England and on life are focused. As we said,
he unifies the chivalric matter of the poem as his presence bound
the British throughout their chronicled history. But Spenser establishes Arthur's importance even before the reader enters the poem.
Twice in the *Letter to Ralegh* the poet emphasizes Arthur's role as
mediator between the world of the poem and the world at large,
as Arthur, like Elizabeth, resists complete containment by the poem,
resists surrendering all his legendary reality to fiction.

. . . I labour to pourtraict in Arthure, before he was king, the image
of a brave knight, perfected in the twelve private morall vertues, as
Aristotle hath devised, the which is the purpose of these first twelve
bookes . . .

And later:

So in the person of Prince Arthure I sette forth magnificence in particular, which vertue, for that (according to Aristotle and the rest) it
is the perfection of all the rest, and conteineth in it them all, therefore in the whole course I mention the deedes of Arthure applyable
to that vertue which I write of in that booke.

It is not important that Aristotle never really devised twelve
private moral virtues in his *Ethics,* or twelve public virtues, as
Spenser goes on to imply; Spenser is saying in effect he will write
a twelve-book poem and, if it goes well, he will write twelve more.
Nor is it crucial that Aristotle does not speak of "magnificence,"
Arthur's virtue. In the *Ethics,* Aristotle does discuss Magnanimity
and that is what Spenser means. What is Magnanimity? We find a
good working definition by Sir Thomas Elyot in his famous *The
Boke named the Governour* (1531). Magnanimity means "good
courage," says Elyot and is the companion of Fortitude:

an excellencie of mynde / concernynge thynges of great importance
or estimation / doynge all thynge that is vertuous for the achievynge
of honour. (Book III, chapter 14, fol. 208^{r-v})

For Elyot, Magnanimity is "the garment of vertue," (fol. 209ᵛ) and that is Spenser's Arthur, he who "is the perfection of all the rest, and conteineth . . . them all," the fabulous historical presence who sustains the poem but is not fully contained by it. In this, Arthur is at one with Elizabeth, both vast figures that resist total transformation into images in a poem. Through the two eyes of history and myth, Spenser has seen them both, and his poem is the pursuit of that forest dream, that vision.

PART TWO

ᵉᵍ VII ᵉ

PATTERNS IN THE POEM

To read *The Faerie Queene*, the reader must relax. He must take it as it comes. I do not mean the reader ought to be lulled; the poem will require, indeed, will demand, his closest attention. But because *The Faerie Queene* is not a novel, he must not strain after meaning in the characters, or even expect "characters," in the sense that we find them in prose fiction. The meaning of the poem is in the reader, in the way he lives his life. Spenser is guiding us through a process of growing self-awareness; he is urging us to use what is within, all the levels of our minds, and all the mind at once.

One must learn as a reader to discriminate, to be flexible and tolerant. This is what the poem, to which nothing is alien, in which the unity is finally imaginative, is telling us. Be alive and open, for the poet is fashioning you as he fashions the poem. Hence, by "relax" I mean be malleable and imaginative yourself. Let go; enter the poem and allow the poem to enter you. Allow the poem to work.

The Faerie Queene means to speak to and of the way we live. It is informed, as we know, with that Humanism which believed every private impulse ought to be directed to the common, civic good. In glorifying England, Spenser wanted to relate the best within man to the betterment of mankind. He was deeply concerned with responsibilities to self and the self's responsibilities to others. And he built his poem (with others, I consider it finished) according to the great passage we first noted in Aeneas, of individual to institution.

Thus, Books I and II, Holiness and Temperance, treat the inner man, man unto himself, from Christian and classical points of view. Both (radically Christian) books communicate a basic Spenserian precept: Man only deludes himself; all deception is finally self-deception. In Book I, we learn with Redcross to overcome the illusion of self-sufficiency, or pride; in Book II, we learn with Guyon to recognize the illusions of self-indulgence, to see clearly the monstrosity of using the natural goods of earth and body as ends in themselves and not as means to greater ends.

Books III and IV, Chastity or love and Friendship, consider the individual in relation to a beloved and to other people. Because of the potential variety in such relationships, these books have a much greater episodic structure, a more distinctly "Ariostean" form. And because the potential for misunderstanding and formless multiplicity is increased, the poet is more deeply concerned with themes of balance, with concepts of deep-rootedness, imaged in trees familial and natural, and with themes of containment and ordering ceremony, imaged in girdles and tourneys and marriage.

Books V and VI, Justice and Courtesy, regard man in relation to immediate society and in relation to the whole city of man. Because these are the most public virtues, paradoxically (or humanistically) the emphasis in these books is on securing the soundness and inner wholesomeness of the private man. Artegall must learn to distinguish compassion from pity and to temper justice with mercy, for before society can reflect the lawgiver's conscience, the lawgiver must have brought his inner forces into an ordered and equitable pattern. In Book VI, Calidore cannot be more than the image of Courtesy until he passes through the rigors and travails of his pastoral interlude. The substance of Courtesy is achieved only after Calidore reassumes his armor beneath his shepherd's clothing, finally reconciling in himself the values of country and city. As others have noticed, the three sets of two books each describe the gradual unfolding of a human being's awareness and sense of responsibility: to self, self to other, self to all. The process is similar to the progression from youth to adolescence to maturity, and the poem in this fashion, too, grapples with that essential Renaissance question, the right relation of the One to the Many.

The Faerie Queene is a splendid ceremony about the necessity for ritual, pattern, and ceremony in life, so as to contain and control the demonic forces within and around us all. The poem is about continuity and anarchy and how each reasserts its potency in the path of the other's power. As an image of continuity, Arthur appears often, as we know, but remarkably he reappears in canto viii of every book save Book III and thus initiates the redemptive movement of each book. In III,viii, we do not meet Arthur. Instead, here near the center of the poem, the anarchic forces are most concentrated. Here we first meet that embodiment of illusion and travesty of substance, the False Florimell, and the very principle of deceptive flux, Proteus. Throughout, Arthur seeks the ennobling visionary core of experience; near the core of the poem, vanity and mutable illusion are manifest. The dialectic—or what we called the dual impulse—goes on forever at the heart of epic.

The reader ought to be aware of the grand patterns, the alternations of day and night, dark and light; of the metaphors of health and disease, government and strife, art and nature, time and eternity. He should be alert to the alternating rhythms of birth and decay, garden and city, and to the occurrences of those two crucial words, "ruin" and "moniment." Finally, one must watch for the technique of relevant digression, where a small story or episode or myth, seemingly intruded for no purpose, in fact catches and crystallizes the poem's larger concerns.

Some of the most interesting patterns in the poem result from the repetition of similar episodes or images, with the further result that the poem (and reader) acquire ever expanding perspective, increasingly dense versions of experience. For instance, the monster Error (I,i,14) is repeated in Duessa's "many headed beast" (I,viii,6;16) and again in the great Dragon (I,xi), each version of monstrosity summing up and enriching the previous one. So also the boar imprisoned by Venus in a cave (III,vi,48) in its way foreshadows the snake beneath Venus' feet (IV,x,40), the crocodile subdued in Britomart's dream at Isis Church (V,vii,6), or the lion under Mercilla's throne (V,ix,33). Again, the beast that feeds on women, released by the Witch from a cave (III,vii,22f) prefigures the Blatant Beast whose bite is slander (V,xii,37f), while the Beast's assault on Serena (VI,iii, 24) is an image completed and expanded by the tiger's attack on Pastorella (VI,x,34–35).

In a sinister way, the poem is sustained by the destructive energy contained and released through all these monsters. The poet's powers of formation and re-formation, in an aesthetic and moral sense, seem to draw strength from what the poem abhors, the images and sources of deformation. In typically Spenserian fashion, this particular version of the dual impulse in the poem is made obliquely clear by the reaction of humankind to the beasts among them. When Calidore paraded the leashed Blatant Beast "through all Faery Land," the people gawked and some "much admyr'd [wondered at] the beast" (VI,xii,37). Similarly, after Redcross has subdued the Dragon, the folk came to touch and look and measure it (I,xii,10–11), no more able to resist the shape of evil than was Redcross in the initial episode of the poem when, despite Una's warnings, he sought out Error in her den (I,i,14f). Once we have read the repetitive pattern forward through the poem, we can then read it back and see how history always repeats itself, how men are always drawn to the beasts among them because man is drawn to the beast within him. The people around the Dragon and the Blatant Beast seem to reanimate evil, as Redcross roused Error from her maternal nursing. In *The Faerie Queene,* man is drawn to what he fears most, partially because he must constantly prove himself again, prove himself man and not beast. He must prove himself because since the Fall, the distinctions between him and beasts are blurred, though in proving himself man always, despite himself, reveals how far he has fallen. We ought not be surprised that the Dragon may yet show life (I,xii,10), that the Blatant Beast somehow

> broke his yron chaine,
> And got into the world at liberty againe.
> (VI,xii,38)

In the fallen world, the Dragon of sin and death cannot die, and vicious slander, fallen language used to dehumanize others, cannot be tamed. The struggle against error, against the deformation we brought upon ourselves, is endless.

These comments arise from noting only one repetitive series in the poem. There are other, larger series to note, those of the Houses and the Visions, and in them we may read *The Faerie Queene's* deepest organizing principles.

By a House, I mean any dwelling, from hut, cottage, or dungeon to bower, castle, or palace; I mean any edifice which is an image of containment. Lists would vary; what follows is my version of each book's pattern of Houses:

Book I: Archimago's cottage, i,34; Corceca's cottage, iii,14; Lucifera's House of Pride, iv,4f; Orgoglio's palace, viii,29f; the House of Holiness, x,3f; the Palace in Eden, xii,13f.

Book II: Medina's palace, ii,12f; Alma's House of Temperance, ix,10f; Acrasia's Bower of Bliss, xii,43f.

Book III: Malcasta's Castle Joyous, i,31; the Witch's cottage, vii,6f; Malbecco's castle, ix,9f; Busirane's Palace, xi,21–xii.

Book IV: Castle of concord (Unnamed), i,9f; dwelling of Até, i,20f; "Cottage" of Care, v,33f; the Temple of Venus, x,6f; Proteus' House, xi,9–xii,14.

Book V: Castle of Polente, ii,20f; Radigund's city and castle, iv,35f; Dolon's house, vi,22; Isis Church, vii,3f; Mercilla's Palace, ix,21f; Belgae's City, x,25f; Irena's Palace, xii,25.

Book VI: Malefort, castle of Crudor, i,22f; Castle of Aldus, iii,2f; Hermitage, v,34f; Castle of Turpine, vi,19; Meliboee's cottage, ix,16f; Robbers' place, x,42–xi,24; Castle of Belgard, xii,3f.

At first glance, this seems an inchoate mass, simply a jumbled list. But the reader will discover interesting alternations and rhythms through Spenser's juxtaposition of these concentrated images of the poem's concern with containment. And out of this catalog we may suggest some broad patterns of parallelism and unity within the poem.

There are three major patterns of parallelism among the books. The first is the parallelism between Books I and II; Books III and IV; Books V and VI—the natural parallelism of adjacent books that have "like race to ronne" (II,i,32). Using only the examples of the House and the occurrences of Arthur, we see the following: At the beginning of Book I, Archimago's hut (i), and of II. Medina's castle (ii): in both books, Arthur as saviour in canto viii; in both, the major edifice soon afterward (Holiness, I,x; Alma, II,ix) and then a landscape restored in canto xii. In Book I, the landscape is Eden (so called at II,i,1); in Book II, Eden is "restored" when the Bower of Bliss, a false Eden (II,xii,51) is overturned, and reversal, as so often in this poem, establishes proper order. Contrast between the "like race" of each book also reveals radical similarity, reflected in structure.

Britomart herself binds together Books III and IV. In both, polarities are quickly established—in III, Britomart at another Bower, now Malcasta's (i), in IV, a castle of concord opposed to Até's dwelling (i). In both books, a girl then dwells at the center of a House, the wasted Hellenore at Malbecco's (III,ix), Amoret nourished in womanhood in Venus' Temple (IV,x). And in both books, marriage is the concern at the end: The pressures of courtly society on the bride Amoret are anatomized in the Castle of Busirane (III,xi–xii), while in Proteus' House (IV,xi–xii) the rivers are married and Florimell is imprisoned.

In terms of development, Books V and VI run a very similar race. In Book V, the regression, of Artegall, from Pollente (ii) to Radigund (iv) is balanced in Book VI by the progression in value from Malefort's (i) to Aldus' castle (iii). In both books, canto vi is a low point (Dolon's house in V, Turpine's castle in VI) and in both, canto viii shows Arthur. In V,ix, we have the didactic spectacle of Mercilla's Palace; in VI,ix, the humble example of Meliboee's hut. In canto xii of both books, the Blatant Beast intrudes to undercut the satisfaction of restoring Irena to her land (in V) and Pastorella to her parents (in VI).

The second set of parallels and correspondences between books emerges when we remember Books I–III were published in 1590, and Books IV–VI, and hence the whole poem, in 1596. One can see parallel blocks, with I and IV, II and V, and III and VI occupying similar positions in each block. Again, using Houses and Arthur, interesting patterns are revealed.

In both Books I and IV, canto i establishes discord and strife either in a house (Archimago's cottage, I,i) or by juxtaposition of houses (Castle of concord versus Até's dwelling, IV,i); then Arthur appears in the seventh canto of each book, and the tenth canto reestablishes concord (House of Holiness, I; Temple of Venus, IV). As a result, lovers are betrothed in canto xii (Redcross and Una in I; Marinell and Florimell in IV) and children are reunited to parents (Una to her mother and father; Marinell to Cymoent).

Books II and V, the most "Aristotelian" books, or where the *Ethics* most visibly, if sporadically, intrude, contrast Medina's Castle (II,ii) with Pollente's (V,ii), and then offer the fruitful comparison of Alma's House (II,ix) with Mercilla's Palace (V,ix). In canto xii of both books, the hero and companions undertake a sea voyage in order to rectify a wrong: in II, to destroy the monstrosity, and monsters, wrought by Acrasia, and to restore right regard for the senses; in V, to destroy the monstrous Grantorto and to restore Irena to her rightful seat.

Books III and VI present contrasts. Malcasta's Castle Joyous (III,i) and Crudor's Malefort (VI,i) are clearly similar but the books' concerns diverge when we compare the waste and restlessness of Hellenore in the prison of Malbecco's castle (III,ix) with the wholesomeness and joy of Pastorella in the community around Meliboee's hut (VI,ix). Unease at Malbecco's becomes social and individual disease writ large at the House of Busirane (III,xii), while pastoral integrity at Meliboee's becomes civic and familial harmony at the castle of Belgard (VI,xii).

However, neither the correspondences suggested by "like race to ronne" nor those triggered by the dates of publication are as revealing as the patterns that grow naturally from the core of the poem, the correspondences between Books III and IV, II and V, I and VI. We noted above the way Britomart binds III and IV, the way her presence at Malcasta's (III,i) parallels the opposition between the Castle of concord and Até's house (IV,i); or the way Busirane's House (III,xi–xii) and Proteus' (IV,xi–xii) are scenes for differing versions of marriage—the former ending with the restoration of Amoret to Scudamour, though we never see it, and the latter with the betrothal of Marinell and Florimell. We also saw how II and V were similar: from different kinds of social and individual discord (Medina, II,iii; Pollente,V,iii) to re-integration (Alma,II,ix; Mercilla,V,ix) to restoration of hierarchy and suppression of deformity (Bower to Bliss,II,xii; Irena,V,xii). Books I and VI commence with edifices containing hospitality and deceit (Archimago's, I,i; Malefort, VI,i) and end with festive palaces of bethrothal and generations reunited (Eden palace, I,xii; Belgard, VI,xii).

By referring to "parallels," "correspondences," and "patterns" I have risked making rigid what Spenser always leaves fluid. I have played a game, to be sure, but a game with a point: which is, to demonstrate that flexibility or even fluidity is not formlessness, and that Spenser's genius for conflation, for blurring the edges, does not mean hard centers of meaning and concern are lacking in the poem or that these centers are randomly distributed or that they do not convey accumulating significance. By emphasizing now one element in a canto, now another, we see different movements and meanings emerge; and by turning the lens on the same sample, we affirm again the mix and mingle of experience, the plenitude of implication and design, at any point in the poem. As I have asserted more than once, epic poems focus on that core of experience where our humanity is defined by the opposites it encompasses, and in proceeding from House to House we have marked the way the poem contains the very contradictory impulses that nourish it.

Other, broader perspectives are suggested by our tour of the Houses. For instance, the description of Archimago's cottage:

> A little lowly hermitage it was,
> Downe in a dale, hard by a forests side,
> Far from resort of people, that did pas
> In traveill to and froe: a little wyde
> There was an holy chappell edifyde,
> Wherein the hermite dewly wont to say
> His holy thinges each morne and even-tyde.
>
> (I,i,34)

is very like the description of the Hermit's hut:

> a little hermitage there lay,
> Far from all neighbourhood, the which annoy it may.
>
> And nigh thereto a little chappell stoode,
> Which being all with yvy overspred,
> Deckt all the roofe and shadowing the roode,
> Seem'd like a grove faire braunched over hed:
> Therein the hermite, which his life here led
> In streight observaunce of religious vow,
> Was wont his howres and holy things to bed.
>
> (VI,v,34–35)

In the first hermitage lives the great author of deception, in the second the embodiment of integrity. At the first cottage, Redcross and Una are separated, at the second Tristram and Serena are cured. Wholeness or wholesomeness, as unity and as health, is the basic issue in each place (and in the poem at large), and the surface similarity of the two cottages only emphasizes the radical differences between them. Here is a constant Spenserian technique: the introduction of two separate incidents or descriptions with identical surfaces and opposite meanings. In this way, the poem draws constantly on itself as a reservoir of past history and human experience, always impressing on us—as the poem seems to start over and over—how different substances are from surfaces, and how we must learn to discern the true from the false. In this vast world of *déjà vu*, of repetitive phenomena, of recommencements, only wariness and cumulative experiences will guide us to the single and abiding visionary core.

As these two hermitages make clear, there can be moral progress of a sort; men, and readers, can pass through similar patterns and learn from past history. Despite the hostility of the world, there do exist in *The Faerie Queene* landscape oases of hope. There are hermits who cure wounds and are what they seem. As an index to this redemptive movement in the poem, it is significant that we move from a hut of falsity in the isolated wilderness in I,i, to a castle with a joyous and reunited family in VI,xii. Indeed, the first and sixth books of *The Faerie Queene* both end with a daughter restored to her parents' castle; at the end of Book I, Una is at home in Eden with the King and Queen (Adam and Eve); at the end of Book VI, Pastorella is brought home to Belgard and to Bellamoure and Claribell. The vision of Romance is always restoration of lovers and of lands, the reestablishment of edenic sentiments and landscapes. And in Romance, whether narrative poem or drama, the symbol for the harmony of sentiment and place, and for the wholesome continuity of human and physical nature, is the deeply satisfying reunion of the generations.

Through one other sequence of events, we may see how the poem fundamentally proceeds. That is the sequence of visions. In *The Faerie Queene* great moments of vision are often closely connected with the poem's grand landscapes. Visions occur in I,x, when Redcross sees Jerusalem from the summit of the Mount of Contemplation; in III,vi, when the reader is given a vision of the flux and fecundity of life in the Garden of Venus and Adonis, a kind of unfallen Eden; in IV,x, when Scudamour recounts his vision of Concord in the Temple of Venus; at V,vii, when Britomart has her dream of concord at Isis Church; in VI,x, when Calidore sees Colin

and the maidens on Mount Adicale; and at VII,vi and vii, the Mutabilitie Cantos, which are themselves visions of strife and resolution
between time and eternity, Mutability and Nature.

Three of these massive moments occur in the tenth canto of a
Book (I, IV, and VI) and three in either cantos vi or vii (III, V, and
VII). In the three books where vision occurs in canto x, Arthur first
appears in canto vii, rather than, as in II and V, only in canto viii.
Where vision is later, Arthur comes earlier, initiating the redemptive
and harmonizing impulse. With what we know of Arthur, Houses,
and visions, we may hazard some general statements about the general movement of each book.

Cantos i and ii always establish discord through the activity and
energy in some kind of house, and this disruptive force runs up to
or through the first six cantos in every book. Then, often by canto
vii, always by canto viii (save in III and the incomplete VII), Arthur
appears and begins to restore what has been divided or lost. When
Arthur has not appeared in vii, a vision has; when he does appear
by vii, a vision appears in x. And then in cantos ix or x, a significant
House sums up the aspirations or concerns of the book: The House
of Holiness (I,x) or Alma (II,ix); Malbecco's castle (III,ix) foreshad-
owing the House of Busirane; the Temple of Venus (IV,x), Palace
of Mercilla (V,ix), and cottage of Meliboee (VI,ix).

In each book, canto xii is the canto of restoration and redemption,
of betrothal, marriage, rescue, and right restored. In canto xii, all
the deformations posited in cantos i and ii are reformed—often after
a confrontation with the agent of deformation: the Dragon (I),
Acrasia (II), Busirane (III), Grantorto (V), even the Robbers of VI.
In IV, we see the embodiment of deformation, of shape-changing,
Proteus, act as host to the marriage of the rivers—a splendid image
of the ambiguous nature of the power of transformation, which is
also the poet's power. But we must not anticipate the matter of our
last chapters.

The spirit of reconciliation is powerful and crucial, to be sure, but
not, in this world, always completely efficacious. While it is true that
Redcross and Una in Book I and Calidore and Pastorella in Book
VI pledge love, we never see them married, any more than we see
married Artegall and Britomart, who, we are told, will found a
noble line. And while Scudamour and Amoret are married, their

fortunes display quite the opposite of wedded bliss. Besides Thames and Medway (IV,xi–xii), therefore, the only spousal we witness is that between Marinell and Florimell (V,iii). In earlier books, Marinell and Florimell had figured the deadening and divisive influences of Wealth and Beauty, but nothing is constant in *The Faerie Queene*. This pair's union, following the marriage of the rivers, becomes a figure for the union of the sea (Marinell) and the flower (Florimell), another Spenserian version of the harmony in the natural universe, a harmony each man must find for himself through cultivation of the best in human nature. Spenser is the greatest poet of marriage in English literature, and in many ways *The Faerie Queene* is his greatest marriage poem. But unlike his *Epithalamion* and *Prothalamion*, which celebrated actual nuptials, Spenser's epic celebrates rather the *ideal* of marriage and union in all things while it remains acutely conscious of the obstacles to perfect consummation here below.

Depite these *caveats*, however, the twelfth canto of each book does reveal the deepest tide running through the whole poem, and in many ways canto xii of Book I contains the seeds that will blossom in the other books. In I,xii, a daughter is restored to parents, as also occurs in VI,xii; in I,xii, a land is redeemed and returned to its rightful condition, as happens in II,xii, and V,xii; in I,xii, there is a betrothal very like a spousal, as a bride is redeemed in III,xii, and marriage and betrothal occur in IV,xii. Out of the twelfth canto of the first book comes again that basic set of correspondences, I and VI, II and V, III and IV; and from the same canto come also those basic relationships so sacred in the poem, and so often assailed, the relations of child to parent, lover to beloved, man to his land. Always Spenser hopes for reconciliation; always he seeks the unity of the individual and the group without denying ever what is best in and best for each.

❧ VIII ❧

PAGEANT, SHOW, AND VERSE

In his *Observations on the Fairy Queen of Spenser* (1752), Thomas Warton remarks:

> We should remember that, in this age allegory was applied as the subject and foundation of public shews and spectacles, which were exhibited with a magnificence superior to that of former times. The virtues and vices, distinguished by their representative allegorical types, were frequently personified and represented by living actors. These figures bore a chief part in furnishing what they called *pageaunts;* which were then the principal species of entertainment and were shewn, not only in private, or upon the stage, but very often in the open streets for solemnising public occasions, or celebrating any grand event. . . . [Spenser's] peculiar mode of allegorizing seems to have been dictated by those spectacles, rather than by the fictions of Ariosto. (1807 edition, II,74–75; 76)

Warton, as so often, touches on something very important for *The Faerie Queene.* Certainly there had been pageants before the time of Spenser. In Volume I of the *Variorum* edition of Spenser, the reader will find enumerated the spectacles involving St. George, the dragon, and the King's daughter and her lamb that were presented before or by Henry V and Edward III and that are so reminiscent of the opening and the ending of the first book of *The Faerie Queene.* But Elizabeth's reign saw pageantry, and the enthusiasm for pageantry, reach its peak. Of course, the taste for pageantry did not pass with the coming of a new century and new monarch. Shakespeare's Gower can be sure his auditors have aptly learned to suppose

> What pageantry, what feats, what shows,
> What minstrelsy and pretty din,
> The regent made in Mytilene
> To greet the King.
>
> *(Pericles, V,ii,6–9)*

The spectacles so crucial to the formation of *The Faerie Queene,* and its audience, were those, however, that greeted England's queen wherever she went.[1]

On the innumerable progresses by and pageants for Elizabeth, we can note only two and consider them emblematic of the form and spirit of the rest. These two are the series of images that greeted her on the day before her coronation, held on Sunday, January 15, 1559, and the spectacles presented during her nineteen-day visit to her favorite, the Earl of Leicester, at Kenilworth Castle in July of 1575.[2] In his *Chronicles of England, Scotland and Ireland,* Raphael Holinshed tells of Elizabeth's progress through London to Westminster on January 14, 1559. Holinshed compares London to "a stage" (London edition, 1808, IV, 159f.)—a crucial element in the idea of pageantry. At Fanchurch, a child sang and Elizabeth saw two figures, representing Henry VII and his wife Elizabeth, daughter of Edward IV. This pageant represented "The uniting of the two houses of Lancaster and York," the union of the White and the Red roses after the War of the Roses. The chronicler explains the significance of this scene:

> It was devised, that like as Elizabeth was the first occasion of concord, so she another Elizabeth, might mainteine the same among hir subjects, so that unitie was the end whereat the whole devise shot . . .

In a kingdom divided by religious dissension, disturbed by the questions of royal legitimacy and (increasingly) of royal succession, and threatened from beyond the channel, concord and unity were overriding concerns of the people and their monarch. Concord and unity, as we know and will see, were also the concern of Elizabeth's greatest poets.

At Cornhill, she saw a pageant on "The seat of worthy government"; at Cheape, two shows: Promises of God to People, and A Flourishing Commonwealth. The last representation came at Fleetstreet. Here was a pageant showing Deborah (Judges, 4–5) as a good ruler consulting with her people, another reminder by the citizens of London to their future Queen of their hopes for her and for themselves. At Temple Bar, there was another oration from a child, verses in Latin and English from "Gogmagog the Albion and Corineus the Briton, two giants" that explained the whole procession, and farewell verses from children. Then Elizabeth went to

Westminster where, next day, she took the crown. Deborah had come, the heir to Brut and Arthur, she who would be in the next forty-odd years celebrated under many guises, among them Astraea, the virgin of Justice who fled the earth when the Golden Age ended, and Belphoebe and Gloriana, the Faery Queen.

The passage through London was very much of the people, a progress which displayed their desires for peace and which drew its figures and significance from British and Biblical history. The glittering royal visit to Leicester's Kenilworth Castle in Warwickshire from Saturday, July 9, to Wednesday, July 27, 1575, was a very different occasion. It was aristocratic, chivalric, and complex. A retainer of Leicester's, one Robert (?) Laneham, has left us a famous account of the Queen's visit in his *Letter* (ed. F. J. Furnivall, The New Shakespeare Society [London, 1890]), and there we can see the Queen did not lack for the more traditional amusements and delights, such as morris dancing, bearbaiting, an Italian tumbler, and a play by the Coventry Men.[8] But tournaments, knightings, and "literary" pageants were in the main fare. For instance, upon her arrival in the Castle, the Queen was confronted by

> the Lady of the Lake (famous in King Arthurz book) with too Nymphs waiting vppon her, arrayed all in sylks, attending her highness comming: from the midst of the Pool, whear, vpon a moouabl Iland, bright blazing with torches, she floting to land, met her Maiesty with a well penned meter and matter. (Furnivall ed., pp. 6–7)

The Lady then described the antiquity of the castle and its owner's line and told of her own guardianship of the lake since Arthur's departure.

> This Pageaunt was clozd vp with a delectable harmony of Hautboiz, Shalmz, Cornets, and such oother looud muzik . . . (p. 7)

The delectable harmonies continued unabated throughout the Queen's visit, and though one might assume it a considerable strain never to know when a myth might leap from behind a rock or out of a grove, there is no record to show that the Queen was anything but delighted. Her nerves and her complete recall of her culture's lore were always at the ready as the images and glories of the past maintained a constant parade. Little wonder the Elizabethans so thoroughly enjoyed and understood their theatrical metaphors for life.

In the course of her stay at Kenilworth she was met by numerous classical and mythological deities; by a "Hombre Seluagio, [Savage Man—the woods of Spenser's poem are full of such men too] with an Oken plant pluct vp by the roots in hiz hande, himself foregrone [grown over] all in mos and Iuy" (p. 14), who recited praises of Her Majesty in verses by George Gascoigne (perhaps, Mulcaster) and presented a summary of the events to that point; and at one point the spectacle of

> a swimming Mermayd (that from top too tayl waz an eyghtéen foot long,) Triton, Neptunes blaster: whoo, with hiz trumpet foormed of a wrinkld wealk, az her Maiesty waz in sight, gaue soound very shrill and sonoroous, in sign he had an ambassy to pronoouns. (p. 33)

The only entertainment Laneham says they kept from the Queen was a middle-aged minstrel with versified selections from Malory. Evidently, he was not considered elevated enough.

While the mythological and literary pageants of Kenilworth are more sophisticated than the spectacles presented to Elizabeth in London in 1559, the earlier series of images, enacted as Holinshed said upon the "stage" of the city, is closer to the original meaning (and spirit) of the word *pageant*.

A word of disputed origin, *pageant* derives immediately from the late Middle English *pagyn*, which was contemporary with the Anglo-Latin *pagina*. It is a word with four primary and several secondary meanings. A pageant is (1) a scene acted on a stage, a usage applied particularly to the Mystery Plays (late fourteenth century) with (a) the figurative meaning of a part in the drama of life. This primary meaning is implicit in Holinshed's account of Elizabeth's progress in 1559, and both primary and figurative senses exist in Duke Senior's famous words in *As You Like It*:

> This wide and universal theater
> Presents more woeful pageants than the scene
> Wherein we play in.
>
> (II,vii,137–39)

There is also another subsidiary meaning from the late fourteenth century, *pageant* as (b) a deceit or trick, the meaning conveyed by the Venetian Senator when he says in *Othello* that the Turks only feign an attack on Rhodes:

> 'Tis a pageant
> To keep us in false gaze.
>
> (I,iii,18–19)

The second and third primary meanings of pageant shade into one another. A *pageant* was (2) a stage or platform on which a scene was acted or a tableau presented; it was also (3) any kind of show, device, or temporary structure, exhibited as a feature of a public triumph or celebration, carried on a moving car or erected on a fixed stage. The last primary meaning, which continues 1b and to which we will return, is *pageant* as (4) an empty show, a spectacle without substance or reality.

With the meanings of pageant before us, let us go back to meaning 1a—a scene acted on a stage, used with special reference to Mystery Plays. The Chester Mysteries were called *pagina prima, pagina secunda,* and so on, after the Anglo-Latin root *pagina* for pageant. But Latin *pagina* is also the root of English *page,* and thus *pageant* and *page* derive from the same Latin word.* And, etymology aside, it is certainly true that the content of a public spectacle, particularly in procession, is similar to the content displayed and bound in a book.

Pageantry is a way of writing—one can "write" a pageant because pageantry is a language. It is a way of talking about intensely private

---

* PAGEANT, from Middle English *pagyn, padgin,* contemp. with Anglo-Latin *pagina.* The sense "scene" probably preceded the sense "stage." AL *pagina* is identical with L. *pagina,* and from the Latin come French *page* as well as Fr. literary forms *pagine, pagene,* which come into English as *pagine, pagyn* (*e*), *pagen,* and in the fifteenth century, *pagent*—all identical with *pageant.* PAGE, meaning one side of a leaf of a book, fifteenth century, from Old French *page* (reduction of *pagine*), from L. *pagina,* which means either (a) a page for any writing; (b) a leaf or slab; or (c) four rows of vines joined together in a square, a bed or quarter—hence, a vine-trellis or column of writing. Latin *pagina,* from root *pag* (*pak*) of *pango,-ere,* to fix or to make fast or firm.

There is no difficulty in identifying the forms of *pagina,* pageant, with *pagina,* page. Various conjectures have been offered for the link between the two. It is thought perhaps the meaning of leaf or page of a MS play passed into that of scene or act. Or, if one thinks of "stage" as the earlier sense of pageant, then perhaps *pagina* passed from "tablet or slab" (for inscription) to "board" and thence to "stage." OED, and *Oxford Dictionary of Etymology,* ed. C. T. Onions et al. (Oxford, 1966), s.v. "pageant" and "page."

concerns in a public manner—as in 1559 the people of London spoke to Elizabeth in the streets about their deepest concerns. A single scene or stage, a pageant, is a static moment, but pageants in a series present cumulative and enriching perspectives, as do stanzas in a poem or pages in sequence in a book. Shakespeare, who understood the nuances (and visual uses) of the word *pageant* so well, also perceived the link between *pages* and *pageant,* the way spectacle is a public form of writing (and reading). In *Richard III,* the old Queen Margaret tells the young Queen Elizabeth that once she thought Elizabeth only a poor copy of herself:

> The presentation of but what I was,
> The flattering index of a direful pageant.
>
> (IV,iv,84–85)

In the sixteenth century, *index* had the (now obsolete) meaning of a "table of contents prefixed to a book . . . also, a preface, prologue" (OED). Hence, Elizabeth was only prologue to the book (pageant) that she and Margaret became. Indeed, the three lamenting women—Margaret, the Duchess of York, and Elizabeth—form a pageant of England's decline. They are three hieratic, sorrowful scenes—a public statement about England to be read by the spectator before the light is blotted out by him who will "spy my shadow in the sun" (I,i,26).

To consider pageantry as a public language signifying private concerns is to approach an idea of allegory. For allegory is a way of talking about substances by way of surfaces, a means of focusing on the private, inner, and hidden through the public, available, and open. Such an approach to allegory (or to pageantry) means we must always absorb the surface, the literal level, in order to penetrate to the substance. We must learn to read the public writing of pageantry in order to grasp the common but submerged private significance. In allegory or in pageantry, the surface is never sacrificed to the substance; surface is, rather, at the service of substance. We must learn, as spectators, as readers, to read back from what is available to what is hidden. We must learn to read out of and into ourselves.

Spenser used the term "pageant" in a variety of ways. In his gloss to *"Many Graces"* in the "June" eclogue, E. K., annotator of *The Shepheardes Calender,* says that Spenser wrote a work called *Pag-*

eaunts. It is now lost, but one can assume that some of it made its way into *The Faerie Queene.* In the epic, there are numerous individual pageants: the procession of the Seven Deadly Sins (I,iv,18–37), the Masque of Busirane (III,xii,6–25), Mutability's progress of seasons, months, hours, life, and death (VII,vii,28–41), to name but a few. But we are urged to see whole books as pageants as well. Redcross says to Guyon and the Palmer:

> His be the praise, that this atchiev'ment wrought,
> Who made my hand the organ of His might:
> More then goodwill to me attribute nought;
> For all I did, I did but as I ought.
> But you, faire sir, whose pageant next ensewes,
> Well mote yee thee. . . .
>
> (II,i,33)

Book II and Book I are by implication pageants, and immediately after Redcross's words, at II,i,36, Guyon's adventure begins with one of those "sad pageaunts of mens miseries," the tableau of Mordant, Amavia, and Ruddymane. Later in the poem, the poet muses.

> Wonder it is to see in diverse mindes
> How diversly Love doth his pageaunts play,
> And shewes his powre in variable kindes.
>
> (III,v,1)

Not only is variability and diversity always the subject of the poem, but the matter of Books III and IV is precisely the multiple forms of Love in progressive pageant before (and within) the reader's mind. When in his dedicatory sonnet to Lord Howard, Lord High Admiral, the poet says that Howard is an example:

> Of th' old heroes, whose famous ofspring
> The antique poets wont so much to sing,
> In this same pageant have a worthy place

the whole series of dedicatory poems may be understood as pageants. Finally, however, it is the epic that is the great pageant. To borrow Shakespeare's phrase, the dedicatory sonnets are only the "flattering index" to the public, triumphal procession of England and her founding heroes.

In the *Amoretti,* his sonnet sequence published in 1595, Spenser presents his most traditional and interesting use of the word pageant. This is the first eight lines of sonnet 54:

> Of this worlds theatre in which we stay,
> My love, lyke the spectator, ydly sits,
> Beholding me, that all the pageants play,
> Disguysing diversly my troubled wits.
> Sometimes I joy, when glad occasion fits,
> And maske in myrth lyke to a comedy:
> Soone after, when my joy to sorrow flits,
> I waile, and make my woes a tragedy.

Through the image of the theater, and in the writing of pageants-pages, we catch the sense of "play," of pretense and illusion that animates the whole poem. *The Faerie Queene* is a spectacle of the various moods and modes of a man's life in the theater of the world. Here we, the reader-spectator, sit watching our private self, our inner being, figured forth in public, and readily understandable, terms.

Thus far we have focused on pageants-pages as a public language that is significant and truly indicative of private concerns. I have suggested that pageantry is like allegory, a surface spectacle leading and urging us through itself to hidden areas of individual moral concern. In this way, Spenser's "spectacular" way of writing, his allegorical mode, is admirably summed up by Isis' gesture to Britomart. The idol, inclining her wand,

> with amiable looke,
> By outward shew her inward sense desining.
> (V,vii,8)

Her outward signs truly reveal her inward sense, just as the poet tells the reader that

> Of Faery Lond yet if he more inquyre,
> By certein signes, here sett in sondrie place,
> He may it fynd.
> (II, proem 4)

So pageantry is itself a system of signs, a language, revealing inward sense.

Such a view, however, is only part of the story. From the beginning, pageant also conveyed those subsidiary and, in the sixteenth century, primary meanings of deceit, of empty show, of hollow or false spectacle. This, for instance, is Juliet's meaning when she hears Romeo has wounded Tybalt, and she calls her beloved "Despised substance of divinest show" (III,ii,77). All pageants are shows, but not all shows are true or wholesome, and thus not all pageants are edifying or trustworthy. Let us recall that Puck also produced "pageants," which only proved "What fools these mortals be" (*Midsummer Night's Dream,* III,ii,115).

Pageants can be empty or deceptive as pages (or books) can be deceiving or misleading, as language itself, notoriously unstable, can destroy as well as create. We must school ourselves to recognize the difference between a surface, a pageant, or a word that celebrates something real, and a surface, a show, or a word that only hides a deceptive or empty core. We need to learn, finally, how far to trust pages, or books, or any form of language, by reading the procession of images with an eye to distinguishing surface which misleads from surface which reflects substance.

In *The Faerie Queene,* Spenser gives us ample evidence of the deceptive side of pageantry, ample warning about trusting anyone's pages or words. The word "show" conveys constantly the deceptive side of public activity, or social behavior. For instance, Radigund's maid, Clarinda, is urged by Radigund to woo Artegall for her mistress; thus, "With daily shew of courteous kind behaviour" (V,v,35) she is to go to the knight. Clarinda's "shew" is meant to deceive him; but when she herself becomes enamoured of Artegall, Clarinda's "shew" has obviously deceived her mistress and, in a sense, herself as well. It is a constant motif in *The Faerie Queene* that, as we hear of Cymochles, someone who "deceives, [is] deceivd in his deceipt" (II,v,34), that the trickster is tricked, that falsity always contaminates its source, and that vice is its own reward. The easy moralism of this motif is always qualified, however, by the constant, underlying implication that only evil will defeat evil in this world, that, finally, good is powerless to do more than stand by and watch, and hope.

Of course, we can do more than stand passively by. We can actively press the issue and probe appearances with the mind. Indeed, we must. True Courtesy, for instance, must always distrust show. Therefore, when Calidore sees the sight on Mount Acidale and does not understand it,

> Whether it were the traine of Beauties Queene,
> Or nymphes, or faeries, or enchaunted show,
> With which his eyes mote have deluded beene.
> Therefore resolving, what it was, to know
>
> (VI,x,17)

he presses strenuously towards it, only to have the vision disappear. The rhyme (and episode) are instructive: (enchanted) "show" is rhymed with "know"—the possibility of falsity impels one, properly, to certainty, and yet the quest for knowledge, tragically, leads to loss.

The Knight of Courtesy's instinctive distrust of vanity and appearances results in the shattering of one of the most authentic moments of vision in the poem, and yet Calidore was in a sense correct. One must see face to face, for so much of the world of the poem is reflected through a glass darkly.

> Her purpose was not such as she did faine,
> Ne yet her person such as it was seene;
> But under simple shew and semblant plaine
> Lurkt false Duessa secretly unseene,
> As a chaste virgin, that had wronged beene;
> So had false Archimago her disguysed,
> To cloke her guile with sorrow and sad teene;
> And eke himselfe had craftily devisd
> To be her squire, and do her service well aguised.
>
> (II,i,21)

This pair, whose essence is falsity and whose goal is division and decay, is everywhere. The spirit of Archimago and Duessa is as ubiquitous in this world as their chivalric trappings are commonplace. It is precisely because what they represent is so commonplace, so much a part of us, that one must guard against show. With Arthur, we as readers must learn when to begin "to doubt [our] dazeled sight" (II,xi,40), for as the poet constantly tells us and shows us, "forged things do fairest shew" (IV,v,15). Ideally, we ought to become like him who guards Mercilla's palace:

> To keepe out Guyle, and Malice, and Despight,
> That under shew oftimes of fayned semblance
> Are wont in princes court to worke great scath and hindrance.
>
> (V,ix,22)

His name is Awe. Spenser wants to inculcate in his reader some awe, some mixture of veneration and dread before the world, some wondrous, wary sense that much as the world is holy, much of what it displays is unwholesome.

Like the world, the poem is full of beauty but also of "an outward shew of things that onely seeme" (*Hymn in Honour of Beautie*, 1,1.91). Thus the poem warns against the poem itself. While like Arthur, gazing at the Faery Queen's image emblazoned on Guyon's shield, we should see the "vertue in vaine shew" (II,ix,3), we must also remember this grand pageant of pages can be seen as only a "painted forgery" (II, proem 1). Even Spenser, recognizing how impossible it is to figure forth the glory of his queen, begs her pardon with an ambiguous term:

> That I in colourd showes may shadow itt,
> And antique praises unto present persons fitt.
>
> (III, proem 3)

The poet is always aware that his poem, like that other artifact, Acrasia's Island, may only "painted colours shew" (II,vi,29), though he hopes, like Calidore, our sojourn in the genuine world of Faery will render us wise: never more to delight

> in painted show
> Of such false blisse, as there is set for stales,
> T' entrap unwary fooles in their eternall bales.
>
> (VI,x,3)

Pageant in *The Faerie Queene*, or pageant as *The Faerie Queene*, means both images of the truth and deceptive illusion. So pageantry leads us back to that dual impulse within the poem and, I have suggested, within all epic. But even more, it leads us back to the dual nature of the reader and of reading. As we move through the pages and the pageant proceeds before us, as what happens without also happens within, the reader is a spectator or *voyeur* and protagonist. As a spectator, the reader must shape himself for moral action; as a *voyeur*, he must learn to become a *voyant*, that is, learn to pass from spying at the edges, like Calidore, to seeing at the core, like Colin Clout. As we watch versions of the truth pass publicly without, we need to learn to recognize the private, personal truth within. Great poems are not only relevant to readers; readers must strive to become relevant to great poems. In the mediative activity of reading, we expand our humanity by engaging a world wholly new to us. The double thrust of pageantry is the dual impulse of the poem. As pageant gives either wholesome spectacle or empty show, so the poem, like daylight, "doth discover bad or good" (Vi,viii,51) in us, in the world. Made of words, the poem, like the prophecies of Proteus, is ambiguous:

> So ticle be the terms of mortall state
> And full of subtile sophismes, which doe play
> With double sences, and with false debate,
> T' approve the unknowen purpose of eternall fate.
> (III,iv,28)

In his pageants, and pages, the poet plays "with double sences" because that is his sense of the way life plays with us. And because of these mutable "termes of mortall state," he will finally cry at the end that Mutability's sway

> makes me loath this state of life so tickle,
> And love of things so vaine to caste away.
> (VII,viii,1)

Because of language's, and life's, "tickleness," its instability, the poet by the end will have lost faith in the power of pageants to please and to indicate permanence, and will crave a Sabbath's sight, which is true, a Sabbath's site which is unchanging.

The poet will lose faith in the power of language to encompass and maintain a vision of ideal truth. He will never doubt that his picture of the antique time offers a better guide to life than the present scene but, as Harry Berger has done so much to remind us, Spenser will find it increasingly difficult to maintain his pageants.* He tells us in the proem (1) to Book V that "the world is runne quite out of square":

---

* Books decline in length after II, sharply after III.

> Right now is wrong, and wrong that was is right,
> As all things else in time are chaunged quight.
> Ne wonder; for the heavens revolution
> Is wandred farre from where it first was pight,
> And so doe make contrarie constitution
> Of all this lower world, toward his dissolution.
>
> (V, proem 4)

Images fail. We cannot depend upon a public language if the public is depraved and the language is unstable. To escape the terror and frustration of the play of double senses, the poet goes inward. He places the sources of ethical wisdom less and less in the public vocabulary of pageantry and more and more within man, within the manageable world of his private self. Now Justice, equity, every social act, is to be measured

> according to the line of conscience.
>
> (V,i,7)

So Astraea teaches Artegall, but does not show him—as she might have earlier in the poem. Now, as Artegall tells the Egalitarian Giant:

> in the mind the doome of right must bee:
> And so likewise of words, the which be spoken,
> The ear must be the ballance, to decree
> And judge, whether with truth or falsehood they agree.
>
> (V,ii,47)

Elsewhere the Knight of Justice is not notably concerned with words. But here he speaks for a poet who conceives of language, like law, as fundamental to an ordered human existence, and who is finding words increasingly incapable of playing their traditional, stabilizing public role. The Giant, who would level all hierarchies and distinctions, threatens with his self-serving, rabble-rousing rhetoric the basic institution of language. And as Artegall asserts the primacy of God's law and traditional Christian distinctions, before using force, the poet retreats into the self as the only sanctuary in which to make moral decisions. *The Faerie Queene* enacts before us that gradual loss of faith in public norms which eventually darkens the view of Jacobean dramatists, for instance, where the only choices to be made and acts to be pursued are desperate and private ones. Finally, Milton may have borrowed extensively from Spenser for his gardens and his heavens, but it was Spenser's deepening moral inwardness and his unshakable Christian convictions that attracted Milton most.

In the fifth stanza of the proem to Book VI we are told that Courtesy today is

> nought but forgerie
> Fashion'd to please the eies of them that pas,
> Which see not perfect things but in a glas.

Now Courtesy is simply chic, and only important to those who see indirectly rather than face to face. It is interesting only to the *voyeurs,* not the seers:

> But Vertues seat is deepe within the mynd,
> And not in outward shows, but inward thoughts defyned.
>   (VI, proem 5)

All is forgery that is not within. The mind is the source and seat of virtue; there exists no longer a public system to communicate a common morality, no longer an "outward shew . . . inward sense desining" (V,vii,8). Spenser has come to the end of pageantry as it extends to allegory, and Book VI is not "allegorical" in the way earlier books were. No great pools of significance gathered around a Despair, or Charissa, or Mammon, or Alma, or Garden of Venus and Adonis, or Busirane, or marriage of rivers; now a story after the courtesy books and Greek Romances, with one great vision but all ethical wisdom, all virtue, deep in the minds of solitary hermits and shepherds. Only the Blatant Beast remains as an impulse from the earlier parts of the poem. And this remnant of the pageantry of the past serves only to embody the harsh truth that no matter how deep in the mind the line of conscience or the doom of right, no matter how far into the self one drives the self, language always bears within it the seeds of monstrosity as well as beauty. As long as men use words, they must risk letting slip the Beast.

Perhaps this view of pageantry and pages overstresses the dark side of Spenser's sense of language. What, after all, kept him writing with any sense of accomplishment if his view of the present state of life was so melancholy, and his faith in words to sustain a better vision so frail? Why did not he cease before he did?

The answer may be partly that for Spenser, in his own particular form of exile in Ireland, writing had become somehow synonymous with living. The long poem, instinct with a better time, peopled with the glistening creations of his imagination, sustained him despite the profound disappointments and frustrations of creating and living. To stop one would have meant stopping the other. That the attraction of ceasing was strong is attested by the temptation to give in that assails his epic protagonists; that he saw no final reconciliation of the images in his head and what he saw around him, or even what he could write, is evident from his own words and from the fact that all ideal moments of vision vanish and all the lovely ladies and brave knights meet only to part with promises of future bliss.

The poem must have filled his life as he put all his humanity into it; its ideal landscapes must have become the far country of his mind, deep in the interior of his being. Certainly he saw the poet as a gardener, working the soil of the soul, a sovereign planter reordering his own inner paradise. From the beginning of his career, Spenser had understood what it meant to write a verse; that is, he knew the English word *verse* was derived from Latin *versus*, the past participle of *vertere*, "to turn," meaning the turn of a plow, a furrow, line or row.* Hence (as we know from pageant and page), a line of verse was the mark of the poet on the page, similar to the mark of cultivation made by the ploughman in the earth. If a page is a plot of land, growing its vine-trellis of writing, Spenser is the careful husbandman, tending, pruning, arranging.

Spenser began early to exploit the radical meaning of "verse." In *The Shepheardes Calender*, after Cuddie sings a complex *sestina* composed by Colin Clout, Perigot says:

> O Colin, Colin, the shepheards joye,
> How I admire ech turning of thy verse!
> ("August," ll. 190–91)

---

* See p. 82, where a *page* is a "vine-trellis or column of writing"—all part of the radical concept of writing as cultivation, art as the working of Nature.

Later he muses on how difficult it is to cram every furrow with the seeds of all he knows. In the midst of narrating the marriage of Thames and Medway, the poet pauses:

> How can they all in this so narrow verse
> Contayned be, and in small compasse hild?
>
> (IV,xi,17)

And yet the small space, or the container, rammed with life's plenitude and energy, is the basic image of *The Faerie Queene*, and here the "narrow verse," the furrow, swells with the names of rivers, is irrigated with the very stuff of life.

Finally, the poet-planter wished to leave no plot unturned.

> Now turne againe my teme, thou jolly swayne,
> Back to the furrow which I lately left;
> I lately left a furrow, one or twayne,
> Unplough'd, the which my coulter hath not cleft:
> Yet seem'd the soyle both fayre and frutefull eft,
> As I it past, that were too great a shame,
> That so rich frute should be from us bereft.
>
> (VI,ix,1)

He then returns to the story of Calidore; he returns to his main "plot."

Spenser did not stop writing for the reason that cultivation of his poem was cultivation of his mind. Public language could become increasingly difficult to sustain; the conviction would grow that virtue lived only deep within the individual mind. But he would never abandon language, or the mind itself. He continued to sow in that green place, continued to turn the soil of his page, and as long as he did, there could be, in the mind and in the poem:

> continuall spring, and harvest there
> Continuall, both meeting at one tyme.
>
> (III,vi,42)

❧ IX ❧

INWARD SOUND

Through pageantry, we watched Spenser manipulate a public mode of writing about private concerns and saw the allegorical perspective on the inner through the outer give way to an emphasis totally on inwardness and interiority. We observed the poet retire to a country seat of the mind. It would be a mistake, however, to assume that the stress on inwardness is a feature only of the last two books. The inwardness at the poem's end that is the narrator's sole perspective has also been a controlling term, and concern, of the poem from the outset.

The terms are established immediately. In I,i, Redcross and Una take shelter in a forest (8–9). They pass every conceivable species of tree, the last of which is "the maple seeldom inward sound." Spenser is here echoing himself, for in the *Ruines of Rome*, translated from Du Bellay, Spenser had spoken of the oak, its "trunke, all rotten and unsound" (stanza 28). The inward unsoundness of trees, and men, is a sign of disease and, in the case of men, of their evil. Spenser indicates the health, and virtue, of nature and human nature by inner soundness, and throughout *The Faerie Queene* rootedness and inner plenitude, the sap of being, are indices to moral virtue. The poet conceives of decency and health in organic, one could say cellular, terms. And where communion with self and nature is absent, where man or tree has lost the vital "excellence / Of his creation, when he life began" (II,xii,87), when because of the Fall man is totally uprooted, then he is void, an empty show, a morally blighted and inward unsound member.

The terms inner soundness and unsoundness echo throughout the poem. After his falsely inspired dreams are allayed and his sleep is restful, Redcross partakes of "sound repast" (I,ii,44), wholesome dreams worthy of Una, not duplicitous dreams that would (and ultimately do) lead to Duessa. Redcross is for the moment sound within his head, nourished by wholeness. But integrity will pass, as all will pass:

> But all is vaine: no fort can be so strong,
> Ne fleshly brest can armed be so sound
> . . . .
> Nothing is sure that growes on earthly grownd.
>
> (I,ix,11)

Arthur's melancholy words recognize that no soundness can survive the Fall or its continual reenactment in the life of man.

Man's fallen mind can be both source and symbol of inner unsoundness. Recall, for instance, Arthur's and Guyon's visit to the chamber of Phantastes (Imagination) in the tower, or head, of Alma's Castle, where flies, like bees, buzz around the room:

> All those were idle thoughtes and fantasies,
> Devices, dreames, opinion unsound,
> Shewes, visions, sooth-sayes, and prophesies;
> And all that fained is, as leasings, tales, and lies.
>
> (II,ix,51)

Imagination can render man, his head, the world, unsound—simply another instance of the way a man is misled only by himself. Book II of *The Faerie Queene* examines the way a man particularly misleads himself as he pursues the illusion, the idle thought and fantasy, of sensual self-indulgence. Especially if he follows Maleger, an existence of malignant passion and desire, who is

> Full large . . . of limbe, and shoulders brode,
> But of such subtile substance and unsound,
> That like a ghost he seem'd, whose graveclothes were unbound.
>
> (II,xi,20)

Book II is devoted to reestablishing sensual soundness, the vitality of the body and its senses, and to dispelling the illusion that sensuality, and specifically sexuality, is an end in itself and not a means to greater ends, like procreation. But because "so feeble is mans state, and life unsound" (II,xi,30), because since the Fall the senses have been exalted to ends in themselves, the battle is constant.

Even the best men, in certain situations, become unsound. The situations are usually amorous ones. For instance, when Timias, Arthur's squire, succors Belphoebe, a Diana attacked by foresters, he becomes an Adonis who is wounded in the thigh. Now she must help him:

> She his hurt thigh to him recurd againe
> But hurt his hart, the which before was sound.
>
> (III,v,42)

Much of Book III is here—in the ironies, and inner unsoundness, of misapplied love:

> Still as his wound did gather, and grow hole,
> So still his hart woxe sore, and health decayd.
>
> (III,v,43)

Why is loving Belphoebe not wholesome, but rather inwardly destructive? Because she is a Diana, not a Venus; she is devoted to that extreme of chastity which is virginity, an ideal totally acceptable but available to very few. (Spenser, after all, could not offend England's Virgin Queen.) It is unsound passionately to love Belphoebe because such love must be fruitless; it can have no issue. Belphoebe was raised by Diana in "perfect maydenhed;" her sister, Amoret, was raised by Venus, in the Garden of Venus and Adonis in "goodly womanhed" (III,vi,28), and it is Amoret, the "lodestarre of all chaste affection" (III,vi,52) who exemplifies the potential for fruitful, married love.

The story of Amoret and Scudamour figures the terrible pressures put upon women by lovers and by society—both forces which are figured in the masque of Cupid in the Palace of Busirane. It is a tale of torments suffered by a woman as she strives to adjust to the expectations of others and to the demands of herself. And it is a story told essentially in terms of soundness.

We first hear of it when Scudamour complains to Britomart that his bride is now seven months the prisoner of Busirane:

> Whilest deadly torments doe her chast brest rend,
> And the sharpe steele doth rive her hart in tway.
>
> (III,xi,11)

Her inner division is the torture partly created by Scudamour's importunate, inexperienced brashness, his over-boldness, but even more by courtly society's easy assumptions about, and subjugation of, women. But when Britomart rescues Amoret from the vast, empty world of courtly forms and conventions, and allows Amoret to earn some true sense of herself, then

> The cruell steele, which thrild her dying hart,
> Fell softly forth, as of his owne accord,
> And the wyde wound, which lately did dispart
> Her bleeding brest, and riven bowels gor'd,
> Was closed up, as it had not beene bor'd,
> And every part to safety full sownd,
> As she were never hurt, was soone restor'd.
>
> (III,xii,38)

The restoration of full inner soundness is the poem's goal. Spenser wants to restore the inner wholeness (or holiness or wholesomeness) of man by removing the knife which divides the heart. In all of us, the tail of Error, of moral wandering, has fixed its "mortall sting" (I,i,15). The poet would have us imitate Redcross who, fighting the Dragon, "strove to loose the far in fixed sting" (I,xi,39)—it makes no difference whether the "sting" be of lust (II,xi,13; III,viii,25; IV,ii,5) or of envy (IV,ii,26) or of infamy (VI,vi,1). His poem, like Britomart, can chart the way to health, but we, like Amoret, must cure ourselves if we are to be truly whole.

Soundness or its absence is the perspective to the end. At the opening of Book VI, we are told that Calidore was esteemed by all at Faery Court "For his fair usage and conditions sound" (VI,i,3). Spenser always establishes a knight's qualities early, not because the knight is in full possession of those qualities but so that the reader will know what the qualities are and what the knight should, and will, be. Thus, once the soundness of Calidore's courtesy is asserted, we are better able to appreciate the way Calidore succumbs to error, to that pastoral wandering among the shepherds which is so necessary to confirm and strengthen his inner qualities and his innate civility. The pattern of loss and restoration of wholeness is fundamental to each of the poem's books, but we can see the pattern, traced in terms of soundness, clearly in Book VI.

The pattern is established early for the reader. Calidore comes upon a woeful squire, hears of the incivility of Briana and Crudor, and then leaves the squire "With hearts dismay and inward dolour queld" (VI,i,18). Later, Calidore battles Crudor and then leaves with his own wounds "hole and strong" (VI,i,47). He will always leave others inwardly sound, because he is the courtly redeemer. Before he departs, however, Calidore reconfirms the lapsed Crudor in his knighthood (VI,i,42–43), as later he will "dub" Tristram his squire (VI,ii,35). At this point we begin to see how, through Calidore, Courtesy is a kind of secular sacrament, a public means for revealing a native, social grace. Much later, even the Salvage Man will knight himself by donning Calepine's abandoned Armor at VI,v,8; one can baptize oneself in the faith of courtesy if one already possesses innate, sound civility.

From an unnamed lady, Calidore hears of a girl and her knight who were attacked by the lady's escort (VI,ii,16–22). The hero then hears the same story from the girl herself, Priscilla (VI,ii,43), and together they carry the wounded knight, Aladine, to his father's house. Priscilla is tormented by Aladine's serious condition and also

> inly did afflict her pensive thought,
> With thinking to what case her name should now be brought.
>
> (VI,iii,6)

The fate of her reputation also tortures Aladine "inwardly" (VI,iii,11) and their concern is "How to save hole her hazarded estate" (VI,iii,12). This mutual inward unsoundness is cured when, by subterfuge, Calidore restores Priscilla to her father (VI,iii,19).

The pattern of a fall from society's grace and a restoration through Courtesy is repeated again, with the same courtly types but larger implications. Book VI proceeds on a pattern of ever ascending spirals of significance. Calidore now meets another knight and lady—a mirror scene, for this couple recalls Briana and Crudor; Tristram and his lady; and Aladine and Priscilla, whom we had met directly as well as through the unnamed lady's recital. This latest pair is Calepine and Serena, whose story will engage us intermittently throughout the book. In the ascending scale of courtly couples (and courtly values), Calepine and Serena stand just below Calidore and Pastorella. Book VI, the story of Calidore, mirror of Courtesy, is told through mirror scenes, each scene projecting a more elevated version of the ideal couple.

> Calepine and Calidore talk, while Serena
> Allur'd with myldnesse of the gentle wether,
> And pleasaunce of the place, the which was dight
> With divers flowres distinct with rare delight,
> Wandred about the fields, as liking led
> Her wavering lust after her wandring sight,
> To make a garland to adorne her hed,
> Without suspect of ill or daungers hidden dred.
>
> All sodainely out of the forrest nere
> The Blatant Beast forth rushing unaware,
> Caught her thus loosely wandring here and there,
> And in his wide great mouth away her bare.
>
> (VI,iii,23–24)

Like the Redcross Knight in another green place (I,vii,7), Serena has been careless of her health and of her fame. Here Spenser pictures her as if she were Proserpina in Enna's field (Ovid, *Metamorphoses* V, ll. 382–408; Claudian, *De Raptu Proserpinae* II, ll. 71–112) or Eve in Eden, snatched away to the detriment of man by the dark, demonic force. The larger mythic perspective, *those* girls behind *this* girl, reveals the pattern of the romance of Book VI, and of the whole poem—a pattern of restoring the effects of the Fall. Only now, because of the initial Fall, man is destined constantly to reenact the restorative process. Now, all women, from Una to Serena, are like Eve, and all the knights are versions of the Redeemer.

Calidore pursues the Beast, who has dropped the girl; for he must try to curb the tongue of rabid speech and save her name, and the fame of mankind. We will not see him again for six cantos. Serena, desperately wounded and separated from Calepine, is cared for by one of the many "salvage" or natural men in the poem. But he can do nothing about her wound, "for it was inwardly unsound" (VI,iv,16). Deep in the woods, with the wild man, Serena has become like the maple at I,i,9—a natural thing whose inner health is lost.

She can be cured only in the Arcadia of the Hermit, where his applications of Stoic advice regarding the need for discipline, restraint, containment, and the "wholesome reede of sad sobriety" (VI,vi,5) allows her to begin to regain her own inner integrity. Again, as with Britomart and Amoret, part of the lesson is that, with help, one must cure oneself to be truly healthy. The fundamental pattern of restoration to civilized self through pastoral hardship is ultimately enacted by Calidore and Pastorella. After the robbers wreck the pastoral world of Meliboee and steal Pastorella, Calidore reconciles his chivalric and pastoral selves by searching for her dressed "in shepheards weeds" while "underneath . . . armed privily" (VI,xi, 36). Now he is literally "inward sound," as the garments of country peace are informed by the armor of courtliness. In Courtesy, as throughout the life of the Renaissance, nature is at its best when reenforced by art.

Pastorella, in the robbers' cave, has fallen brutally from her ideal world, and, as in all fallen beings, "Her sickenesse was not of the body, but the mynde" (VI,xi,8). After her redemption by Calidore and restoration to her parents, however, "the damzell gan to wex more sound and strong" (VI,xii,11). Calidore leaves, as all knights must leave in this poem, to pursue his quest. The process is endless, and the poem ends.

Of necessity, much has been omitted from this sketch of inner soundness, or its absence, in *The Faerie Queene*. The reader will find for himself other instances of this stratum in the poem. To indicate its variety, however, examples of a different sort may be offered.

For instance, the vast, silent emptiness of Orgoglio's and Busirane's palaces (I,viii,29; III,xi,53) is an index in both places to the hollowness of man's carnality and his pride. Or again, the dungeon Redcross inhabits is simply a version of the dark void of potential despair that inhabits him (I,viii,38). In all these cases, Spenser uses the image of a house or dwelling to mirror deadly vacuum rather than plenitude. These places are malignancies in the body of the poem, versions of unsoundness that disrupt and decay the vital, cellular health of the landscape—which is also the landscape of a man's inner being.

Nowhere is this larger perspective on inner disease clearer than in the literal hollow recesses of evil in the enchanted ground of Faery. From Error's "den" (I,i,13) to the robbers' "hellish dens" (VI,xi,3), there is a series of dark places, all underground, all Hellish and all sources of the inner unsoundness they also symbolize. Most remarkable are the cave of Sleep (I,i,39–44), home of the desire to give in and give up that assails so many and reservoir whence come Archimago's false dreams; the cave of Night, located out of this world, the refuge of Duessa's ancestress (I,v,20–28); Avernus, the classical hell where Sansjoy is cured of his wounds (I,v,31–44); and the caves of Despair (I,ix,33–54) and of Mammon (II,vii,20–65), both crucial episodes in the poem that mirror each other. In Book III, s-mothering Cymoent carries Marinell to an underwater cave (III,iv,43–44), similar to the cave in which Proteus will hold Florimell (III,viii,37–38). Venus keeps the boar that wounded Adonis in a cave in their garden (III,vi,48), and the Witch maintains the Hyena that feeds on women in her "hidden cave" (III,vii,22). Finally, Até, the very "mother of debate / And all dissention" (IV,i,19) lives in a cave "hard by the gates of hell" (IV,i,20f.). In all the caves associated with women in Books III and IV there is, of course, a comment on the dark and potentially terrible powers of female sexuality.

All these obscure, hollow recesses of evil, however, are also abscesses in the land of Faery, sources of the "far in fixed sting" that poisons human health. From each of these wounds in the earth emanates an impulse that tempts man to make a hollow place of himself, that tempts him to misuse and abuse his spiritual, emotional, and material substance, and to become a monster rather than—as on hilltops—to become a man. As usual, however, each of these caves proves a fascinating place for either reader or protagonist or both. We always, Spenser is saying, find most compelling that which is most repellent. It is an old story.

Opposed to the impulse from the caves is the constant discovery in the poem of inner soundness behind visors and veils.[1] Throughout *The Faerie Queene,* visors are raised, veils fall away, and a face appears. This revelation, almost always described in terms of streaming light, is a vision of substance and plenitude beneath a cover, and is symbolic of permanence or divinity. The priests of Isis Church tell Britomart:

> "Magnificke virgin, that in queint disguise
> Of British armes doest maske thy royall blood,
> So to pursue a perillous emprize,

> How couldst thou weene, through that disguized hood,
> To hide thy state from being understood?
> Can from th' immortall gods ought hidden bee?"
>
> (V,vii,21)

From the immortal gods, nothing can conceal one's true identity
and condition; but for the rest of us, epic protagonists and epic
readers, the "disguized hood" of visor, helmet, or veil must be
raised before destiny, substance, or divinity can be perceived.

We can only indicate some of the many instances of revelation.
In Book V, for instance, Artegall jousts with a knight:

> Eftsoones they gan their wrothfull hands to hold,
> And ventailes reare, each other to behold.
> Tho, when as Artegall did Arthur vew,
> So faire a creature, and so wondrous bold,
> He much admired both his heart and hew,
> And touched with intire affection, nigh him drew.
>
> (V,viii,12)

By raising their visors, Artegall and Arthur replace strife with
concord and establish trust. In recognizing Arthur and his splendid
qualities ("His heart and hew"), Artegall spontaneously draws Arthur to him and becomes, in effect, what his name implies: Arthur's
equal. By this revelation, Britomart's vision of a strong but tem-
pered lover (V,vii,14f.—at Isis Church; III,ii,24f.—in her father's
magic glass) begins to assume reality. The more Artegall resembles
Arthur, the more he approaches the reality of Britomart's ideal.

Most importantly, this motif of raising visors and veils reveals
men as *voyants*, not *voyeurs*—men as seers directly, face to face, and
not as covert spies at the edges of experience. Through this motif,
again and again the drive of the poem to the center, to the bright
and permanent core of existence, is reenacted. Why reenacted so
often? Because life is transitory and the ideal so elusive. Nothing
in the poem is as strong as the desire for permanence; nothing is
as evanescent as its revelation. Like Arthur, man must forever strive
to regain the vision.

Through women, man can see the divine. When Britomart's face
blazes through her raised visor, at III,i,42–43; III,ix,20; IV,i,13; and
IV,vi,19f., her inner soundness spilling from her armor's contain-

ment is described in terms of light, beauty, and divinity. And when, at IV,vi,22, Artegall slashes away her visor and sees her face, he

> fell humbly downe upon his knee,
> And of his wonder made religion,
> Weening some heavenly goddesse he did see.

The mutable life of enchantment is briefly translated to a higher, more stable plane of existence. Artegall has seen what later the shepherds around Pastorella think they have seen when they

> oft rejoyce, and oft for wonder shout,
> As if some miracle of heavenly hew
> were downe to them descended in that earthly vew.
> (VI,ix,8)

For a moment, the vision of miracle can save us from the mutable Romance world of magic.

Of course, as with everything in this poem, the "double sence" is the norm. Raising a visor can also reveal falsity, can reveal unsoundness as well as inner soundness. At I,iii,38, Sansloy "rudely rending up [a] helmet," sees the "hoarie head of Archimago old," he who "in charmes and magick" had wondrous might. We learn again that not all revelations, or versions of revelation, convey divinity when Artegall unlaces the helmet of Radigund and sees a face he thinks "A miracle of Natures goodly grace" (V,v,12). Artegall, like all of us, must learn to be wary wise, to distinguish visions that liberate from those that subjugate.

Through the visor of Britomart, we receive visions of an earthly grace. Beneath veils, we see Heaven directly. When in battles with Orgoglio (I,viii,19) and the Souldan (V,viii,37), the veil falls from Arthur's "sunlike shield" (V,viii,41) nothing earthly can withstand this brilliant symbol of divine power. But it is Una who most often conveys divinity directly. At the beginning of Book I, Una is alone in the woods; therefore, when she removes her fillet, it is specifically for the reader's benefit:

> Her angels face
> As the great eye of heaven shyned bright,
> And made a sunshine in the shady place;
> Did never mortall eye behold such heavenly grace.
> (I,iii,4)

At the end of Book I, others share in that vision. When she removes the wimple "Wherewith her heavenly beautie she did hide" and reveals the "glorious light of her sunshyny face," now Redcross, stunned, "Did wonder much at her celestiall sight" (I,xii,22–23). Though he had known her for some time, he had never truly *seen* her as she was. He had not seen her because his sight was self-regarding, hence defective; but after the vision in I,x, and the battle with the dragon, Redcross was liberated from himself to the point where he could see another, and, through her, God.

Occasionally the "celestiall sight" is so dazzling we could not bear it. So it is with Nature, the veiled woman who ends the poem, as we have it, and balances Una who began it:

> For, with a veile that wimpled every where,
> Her head and face was hid, that mote to none appeare.

> That, some doe say, was so by skill devized,
> To hide the terror of her uncouth hew
> From mortall eyes, that should be sore agrized;
> For that her face did like a lion shew,
> That eye of wight could not indure to view:
> But others tell that it so beautious was,
> And round about such beames of splendor threw,
> That it the sunne a thousand times did pass,
> Ne could be seene, but like an image in a glass.
>
> (VII,vii,5–6)

The hidden face of Nature embodies life's "double sense," for it is said to be at once terrifying and transcendently beautiful. But would not that also be true of the face of God? Nature, veiled like Venus in the innermost place of Concord (IV,x,41), is the source and image of the plenitude, substance, and soundness within us all. From her, eternal and abiding, the poem draws its nourishing values. Whatever "sound repast" we have, whatever sign we have, in this world, of the next, springs from her multiform and uniform self. "All things not rooted well will soone be rotten" (IV,i,51), we are told; in Faery Land, or anywhere, one must be deeply rooted to be whole and sound. But when a man is deeply rooted, then he will be "fed with heavenly sap" (VI,iv,36): the thick, viscous light of life will swell and replenish his soul, and the armor of his body, and his self. Then he will have achieved the condition of Dame Caelia, at the sight of Una and Redcross, whose "heart with joy unwonted inly sweld" (I,x,8). This is the most sublime condition for a man in *The Faerie Queene,* to feel the spontaneous surging of joy within because the radical self is nourished by Nature and Heaven. Redcross at Dame Caelia's "now grew in litle space" (I,x,21), but readers, as well as protagonists, of epic may begin to fill the space within with soundness. Spenser hopes that his readers too will be deeply rooted in Nature, for her secret visage is discernible after all, even though as "in a glass." The poem is that glass, the poem which holds all the double senses, the good and ill, light and dark, beautiful and terrifying. If we remove the veils from our eyes, the poet will direct our glance directly in, there to see our selves revealed. Throughout *The Faerie Queene,* subtly but insistently, the poet is urging us to sink roots in his art and so within to nurture our natures and grow in soundness.

❦ X ❧

POETRY AND THE POET

Thus far, my emphasis has been on the "double sense" of *The Faerie Queene*; on the dual impulse within epic, the ambiguous nature of pageantry, the language and images of inner soundness and unsoundness. I have suggested that the poem proposes divisions and strives to reconcile them, and that duality and marginality, on the one hand, and the drive to reunion and centrality, on the other, have been the poem's double perspective on life. In short, I have been claiming *The Faerie Queene* is constantly trying to solve the problems of duplicity that are embodied in the poem.

As suggested at the outset, the poem knows everything about the dangers and glories of poetry. It knows poetry is an image of a higher reality and it knows poetry is a lie. It knows poetry can heal your wounds and it knows poetry can corrupt. Rather, the poet knows these things. The self-consciousness is Spenser's; he is the one, especially in the proems to the last two books, who so profoundly questions the power of poetry to shape life for the better. Spenser is obsessed with the problem of division—in consciousness, in the heart, in poetry—because as a poet he is so acutely aware of the ambiguous, that is, mutable and multiple, shapes of words.

Above all, language and its consequences are anatomized in the poem. This vast structure of words returns over and over to the power of words—words as they are the fundamental source and symbol of life's "double sense." As a word is mutable, as a word is real, as a word is insubstantial, so is life and art. By language, we make and are made; we name and we pass on what we know. But language is only a system of symbols, not a set of solid objects. Since the Fall, words have not been things; they merely indicate things. Words themselves are no-thing. But without words, are there things? Is not reality created by words? Was not the world made by a Word, as it says at the beginning of the Gospel of John:

In the beginning was the Word, and the Word was with God and the Word was God.

And do not poets make their worlds of words, in imitation of the Maker whose art is Life? The problem in life is the problem in language: The true and the false, the real and the illusory, the power to heal and the power to kill, are contraries united in our single existence. Our humanity is defined by the opposites it includes, and words, by which we know ourselves and others, both contain those contraries and loose them on the world.

For Spenser, the poet's power is an awesome one: With his fallen speech, he can imitate God and make a new golden reality; or he can fashion a lie and be brother to Satan. Through words, the poet can deform or reform, for language is essentially the power to form, and as we form with words, so we perform in life. Words can impair or repair as Spenser says, punning on the problems of paring / pairing—dividing and making whole. We remember Una who "Is from her knight divorced in despayre" (I,iii,2) as the false words of Archimago have pared her from Redcross and brought despair. Later, Una and Arthur will exploit both the implications of the radical *pair* and finally the implications of language to ruin and restore.

> "But griefe," quoth she, "does greater grow displaid,
>   If then it find not helpe, and breeds despaire."
> "Despaire breeds not," quoth he, "where faith is staid."
> "No faith so fast," quoth she, "but flesh does paire."
> "Flesh any empaire," quoth he, "but reason can repaire."
>   (I,vii,41)

The ills that flesh breeds and the balm faith and reason bring both reside in the double sense of *pair*. One is never free of duality, here or anywhere else. Little wonder that throughout his poem, Spenser returns constantly to the aweful energy of language to create and to destroy, most often through images of the imagination and language, and versions of the poet.

I

We return for the last time to that model of the mind in the poem, the top of Alma's castle in Book II, canto ix. As we remem-

ber, Guyon and Arthur are guided by Alma through three com-
partments wherein "there dwelt three honorable sages" (II,ix,47).
They represent the three dimensions of the mind:

> The first of them could things to come foresee;
> The next could of things present best advize;
> The third things past could keepe in memoree. (49)

The first, the prophet, is called Phantastes (Imagination), and
his room, we recall, was filled with buzzing flies, like bees around a
hive:

> All those were idle thoughtes and fantasies,
> Devices, dreames, opinions unsound,
> Shewes, visions, sooth-sayes, and prophecies;
> And all that fained is, as leasing, tales, and lies (51)

The chamber of Imagination is filled with the products of the
imagination. And the chamber's walls tell us even more about the
nature of the inhabitant:

> His chamber was dispainted all with in
> With sondry colours, in the which were writ
> Infinite shapes of thinges dispersed thin;
> Some such as in the world were never yit,
> Ne can devized be of mortall wit;
> Some daily seene, and knowen by their names,
> Such as in idle fantasies doe flit:
> Infernall hags, centaurs, feendes, hippodames,
> Apes, lyons, aegles, owles, fooles, lovers, children, dames. (50)

A fascinating catalog of the monsters the mind creates—a list that
would repay close study. But what is finally at issue here is Spenser's
portrait of the Imagination and its powers. For Spenser, the imagination was "fantastic," not "icastic," a distinction the Renaissance
found in Plato's *Sophist*.[1] That is, the imagination imitated by
feigning new realities, not by holding the mirror up to Nature. For
Spenser, the fantastic imagination occupies the foremost part of
the human mind; it is the wellhead of the marvelous, the source
of the power to form. And here, where energy is constant and elements constantly take and lose shape, we have Spenser's clearest
version of the power that the artist taps in order to fashion his

artifacts, and we have Spenser's clearest vision of the potential for deformation that is implicit in the process of transformation. This is the Vulcan cave of the poet's psyche, where he forges the monsters he must contain. The other two parts of the mind receive less detailed description, probably because they impinge less on Spenser's particular obsessions with the poetic faculty. Alma next shows her guests a room whose walls

> Were painted faire with memorable gestes
> Of famous wisards, and with picturals
> Of magistrates, of courts, of tribunals,
> Of commen wealthes, of states, of pollicy,
> Of lawes, of judgementes, and of decretals;
> All artes, all science, all philosophy,
> And all that in the world was ay thought wittily. (53)

The unnamed inhabitant, "a man of ripe and perfect age" (54), is the principle of judgment, of "wit"—in short, the capacity to discriminate and then integrate experience into significant patterns. We have moved from the realm of the individual imagination to that of institutions; from fantasy to civility; youth to maturity— the one to the many. In this chamber of civil fullness, the chaotic energy of imagination's den is ordered and arranged. This is the world of "artifice," those things—systems, institutions, codes, conventions—by which we live and which we call civilization. Artifice is, here as throughout the Renaissance, what is most real. It is noteworthy that the first artifact mentioned on the walls is depictions of the memorable deeds of "famous wisards." The world of civility has absorbed the impulses from Phantastes' chamber—for what was that but a magician's den?—and has integrated that energy into the systems of law and conventions of order. In passing from that room to this one, we have, in the terms of another triadic version of the human psyche, passed from the id to the ego.

The third chamber belongs to "that old man Eumnestes" (58), and is the chamber of Memory. Here all that was, is contained.

> His chamber all was hangd about with rolls,
> And old records from auncient times derivd,
> Some made in books, some in long parchment scrolls,
> That were all worm-eaten and full of canker holes. (57)

Here Guyon and Arthur find their books, *Antiquitee of Faery Lond* and *Briton Moniments*; here what the mind has made binds the mind together. Like the poem, the chamber of Eumnestes contains all—myth and history, the fantastic and the civilized. Like the poem, age contains both youth and maturity. Single images and collective institutions are preserved here for posterity. This is the place in the mind that conserves and oversees, a super-ego that protects the whole. This is the part of the mind that stores what the mind has learned, the detached part that supervises engagement throughout. It is the most vulnerable room in the mansion, first prey to mutability and decay. It is the part of us that not first but finally loves *The Faerie Queene*.

Youth, maturity, age; imagination, civility, memory; prophecy, legality, chronicle—one could multiply triads for some time. The point is that Spenser has created a model of the mind and sees the mind as an artifact, containing all. In the specific terms of the poetic or artistic faculty, his model shows us the three stages of aesthetic creation: in the first chamber, the process of imaginative creation; in the second, the products of that process; and in the third, perspective on those products. Whether we look upon the creations of the mind as they are poetic or political or religious, our perspective on them includes a view of them in process and as products. The long view of Eumnestes is the epic's view—it sees how our existence contains within itself both monsters and monuments.

II

It is at the level of language that Spenser most often explores life's "double sense." In his view of words throughout the poem, we come closest to Spenser's preoccupations with creation and decay that were abstractly portrayed at the top of Alma's castle. First we will consider his overall view of language and then see how it is embodied in various figures for the poet in the poem.

Radigund wants her maid Clarinda to woo Artegall for her. Say and do what you will, says the Queen:

> Leave nought unpromist that may him perswade,
> Life, freedome, grace, and gifts of great availe,

With which the gods themselves are mylder made:
Thereto adde art, even womens witty trade,
The art of mightie words, that men can charme.

(V,v,49)

If all else fails, use force, says Radigund. She never says how, but
in this fallen world she recognizes, with everyone else, that a word
is no longer a deed. To want is not to have. Here is Spenser's view
of language, language as rhetoric, a cunning system fashioned to
render the hearer malleable. Words are "charms," that is, a word
is a *carmen,* a song or incantation. To be "charming" with words
means to enchant and bewitch. Basically, Spenser's view of language
is a magical one.

We hear this note again after Redcross has described the nobility
of Artegall to Britomart. She is greatly pleased:

Hart that is inly hurt is greatly eased
With hope of thing that may allegge his smart;
For pleasing wordes are like to magick art,
That doth the charmed snake in slomber lay.

(III,ii,15)

Language can soothe the snake that gnaws us within and renders
us unsound. But language can also, as we will see, summon the
snake and loose him. The pleasing magic can work for good or ill.
It all depends on who is being pleasing, who is the conjuror with
words. It all depends on who is playing the *magus* with language,
who is playing the poet.

The Faerie Queene returns to the figure of the poet often. This
is obvious in the proems and the narrator's intrusions into the
narrative, where we are never allowed to forget the presence of the
poet himself. Sometimes he is a captain mariner navigating the
great ocean of his fiction (I,xii,42), sometimes a pedestrian traveller
(VI, proem 1), sometimes the straightforward chronicler (III,viii,1).
Often he is weary and always he is present. This narrator will also
mention other poets, like Chaucer, "well of English undefyled"
(IV,ii,32), or offer us a persona, like Colin Clout (VI,x,16–30) whose
resigned patience at the intrusion of clownish Calidore reflects the
tone of the narrator throughout.

One of the most interesting references to a poet in the poem occurs, however, when Spenser adduces Orpheus, the greatest poet of the mythological past. Throughout his earlier poetry Spenser had alluded to Orpheus; in *The Ruins of Time,* he had pictured Sir Philip Sidney in the Elysian Fields

> With Orpheus and with Linus, and the choice
> Of all that ever did in rimes rejoyce
>
> (333–34)

and in the *Amoretti,* he remembered

> When those renoumed noble peres of Greece
> Thrugh stubborn pride amongst themselves did jar,
> Forgetfull of the famous golden fleece,
> Then Orpheus with his harp theyr strife did bar.
>
> (XLIV)

though Spenser, as he goes on to say, cannot still the "cruell civill warre" that he makes on himself—an interesting allusion to the divisive "double sense" within the poet. The healing power Orpheus has and the lover lacks in Sonnet XLIV is celebrated superbly in *The Faerie Queene:*

> Firebrand of Hell, first tynd in Phlegeton
> By thousand furies, and from thence out throwen
> Into this world, to worke confusion
> And set it all on fire by force unknowen,
> Is wicked discord, whose small sparkes once blowen
> None but a god or godlike man can slake;
> Such as was Orpheus, that when strife was growen
> Amongst those famous ympes of Greece, did take
> His silver harpe in hand, and shortly friends them make.
>
> Or such as that celestial Psalmist was,
> That when the wicked feend his lord tormented,
> With heavenly notes, that did all other pas,
> The outrage of his furious fit relented.
> Such musicke is wise words with time concented,
> To moderate stiffe mindes, disposd to strive:
> Such as that prudent Romane well invented,
> What time his people into partes did rive,
> Them reconcyled againe, and to their homes did drive.
>
> (IV,ii,1–2)

What Orpheus accomplished among the Argonauts, or the young David before Saul troubled by an evil spirit (I Samuel, 16:23), or Menenius Agrippa when he returned to Rome with Octavius after Caesar's murder, was to heal division and replace discord with harmony. And this constant *desideratum* in the poem—the establishment of wholeness where there had been only doubleness—is accomplished by language, but more specifically by the art of the poet, the god or godlike man. In Orpheus, David, and Agrippa, Spenser projects the poet in all his ancient splendor, as singer, psalmist, and politician, the healer of wounds within and among men. In this light, language used by the good poet can "moderate stiffe mindes," can bring a civilized and civilizing flexibility to the private and the public realms. Here, in the somber wariness of ideologues and ideologies, in the plainly stated faith in the capacity of the good man to use language well to reform men and institutions, is all of Spenser's humanism and his greatest hope for his poem.

We noted above the power of this magic to heal and soothe:

> For pleasing wordes are like to magick art,
> That doth the charmed snake in slomber lay:
> Such secrete ease felt gentle Britomart,
> Yet list the same efforce with faind gainsay:
> So dischord ofte in musick makes the sweeter lay.
>
> (III,ii,15)

But the sweet, shapely harmonies, however arrived at, whether conjured by a Redcross or a Colin Clout on Mount Acidale or an Orpheus, are not the only forms wrought by words. There are also those dark and sinister effects, the snake as summoned and not allayed by words, and we see them clearest in the hags who rend the pure air of the last two books with their foul cries.

In Book IV, canto viii, Arthur, Aemylia, and Amoret come upon a little cottage (23) and its filthy old female inhabitant—much as Una had come upon Corceca's (I,iii,11) and Florimell upon the Witch's (III,vii,6). This crone, "A foule and loathly creature"

> was stuft with rancour and despight
> Up to the throat; that oft with bitternesse
> It forth would breake, and gush in great excesse,

> Pouring out streames of poyson and of gall
> Gainst all that truth or vertue doe professe.
>
> (IV,viii,24)

She is Sclaunder and she is descended not only from the doleful or
deadly crones like Corceca and the Witch, or more obviously from
Duessa, Night, and Até, but also from the more subtle artisans of
language, Archimago, Despair, and Mammon. With her gullet bursting with words, ready to "gush in great excesse," Sclaunder is another version of Error, another creature also primed to release "A
floud of poyson horrible and blacke," a "vomit full of bookes and
papers" (I,i,20)—save in Sclaunder we have come to the very root
of error, to that very source of language as it deforms.

> Her words were not, as common words are ment,
> T' expresse the meaning of the inward mind,
> But noysome breath, and poysnous spirit sent
> From inward parts, with cancred malice lind,
> And breathed forth with blast of bitter wind;
> Which passing through the eares would pierce the hart,
> And wound the soule it selfe with griefe unkind:
> For like the stings of aspes, that kill with smart,
> Her spightfull words did pricke and wound the inner part.
>
> (IV,viii,26)

"Like stings of aspes": Here language does not, as Redcross's did
for Britomart, "the charmed snake in slomber lay" (III,ii,15) but
rather rouses and releases that Satanic part, fixed in us all, which
brings us again and again to fall. Once more the huge shape of
Error lurks behind Sclaunder, for that monstrous asp with a woman's torso, the symbol of all deformity in *The Faerie Queene*, spew-
ing books, spawning "Deformed monsters, fowle, and blacke as
inke" (I,i,22), was the first complex, composite image—we realize in
retrospect—of the bestial, the female, the hideously fallen, finally of
the Satanic power of maliciously misdirected words.

Arthur and his companions endure all "with patience mild"
(IV,viii,28), but the image of the hag and her disfiguring verbal
progeny is indelibly impressed upon us.

We meet another version of Sclaunder again in Book V, where

the implications of the first image broaden. After Artegall has restored Irena to her throne, he

> day and night employ'd his busie paine
> How to reforme that ragged common-weale.
>
> (V,xii,26)

"But ere he could reforme it thoroughly" (27), he is recalled to
Faery Land. But as Gryll had resisted the restoration of his first
shape by the Palmer (II,xii,87), so here there are those who resist
Artegall's efforts to restore a civilized shape to the state. And those
who resist the most are the vile hags Envy and Detraction. Envy
first:

> For what soever good by any sayd
> Or doen she heard, she would streightwayes invent
> How to deprave, or slaunderously upbrayd,
> Or to misconstrue of a mans intent,
> And turn to ill the thing that well was ment.
>
> (V,xii,34)

But Envy, who only vexes herself, is excelled by Detraction:

> Her face was ugly, and her mouth distort,
> Foming with poyson round about her gils,
> In which her cursed tongue full sharpe and short
> Appear'd like aspis sting, that closely kils,
> Or cruelly does wound, whom so she wils.
>
> (V,xii,36)

Again the image of the serpent appears in Detraction's foaming
mouth, but it is Envy, we know, who has been gnawing on a snake
(30) and who now throws it at the receding back of Artegall:

> The cursed serpent, though she hungrily
> Earst chawd thereon, yet was not all so dead,
> But that some life remayned secretly,
> And as he past afore withouten dread,
> Bit him behind, that long the marke was to be read.
>
> (V,xii,39)

The snake, with some life left in him—like, perhaps, that greater
snake in Eden who still lived (I,xii,10)—has been transformed from

the snake in language to the snake of language, language now a
deadly weapon flung savagely at one who would reform society.
Error, the Dragon, the hyena of the Witch—all the beasts and
serpents associated with falsity and deformity through magic and
words—are recalled in the snake Envy and Detraction hurl at Artegall, and the whole monstrous impulse is epitomized in the creature
the hags then loose on Artegall, the Blatant Beast. This monster,
Spenser's supreme figure for the beast in language and for language
put to bestial ends, ranges through Book VI, shredding the courtly
fabric of that romantic world, mocking every effort to contain him,
his rabid bite the essence of slander and lying. He is finally only
restrained when the poet ceases to use language at all.

The radical impulse to deformation in this dark view of language
and its uses runs counter to the heroic faith in the poet's Orphic
power, and to the grand, albeit melancholy, spectacle of Colin
Clout's achievement. The double sense is everywhere, but nowhere
do we sense more clearly Spenser's deeply divided view of the poet
and his material, words, than in Book V, canto ix, outside the
palace of superb Mercilla. Here Artegall, Arthur, and a girl pass by
Order and his company.

> There as they entred at the scriene, they saw
> Some one, whose tongue was for his trespasse vyle
> Nayled to a post, adjudged so by law:
> For that therewith he falsely did revyle
> And foule blaspheme that queene for forged guyle,
> Both with bold speaches which he blazed had,
> And with lewd poems which he did compyle;
> For the bold title of a poet bad
> He on himselfe had ta'en, and rayling rymes had sprad.
>
> Thus there he stood, whylest high over his head
> There written was the purport of his sin,
> In cyphers strange, that few could rightly read,
> *Bon font:* but *Bon,* that once had written bin,
> Was raced out, and *Mal* was now put in:
> So now *Malfont* was plainely to be red;
> Eyther for th' evill which he did therein,
> Or that he likened was to a welhed
> Of evill words, and wicked sclaunders by him shed.
>
> (V,ix,25–26)

Here is Spenser's most chilling version of the "double sense" in language, and of poets. Right before the reader's eyes, he gives us the inextricable mix of good and ill, of *bon* and *mal*, at the heart of his material and his craft. No more literally (or literarily) self-conscious passage exists in the poem than the description of the change in rubric from *Bonfont* to *Malfont*. Here words literally shift and meanings change while the radical element, the source of the poet's art, the *font*, remains the same. Chaucer may have been "The pure well head of poesie" (VII,vii,9) and Malfont "a welhed / Of evill words, and wicked sclaunders" (V,ix,26), but both the pure and the polluted, the good and the evil, tapped the same deep spring, the wellhead in a man's head, the bottomless imagination. From that single source comes all: Orpheus' healing and Sclaunder's deforming, the moments of vision and the divine human faces, and the potent beasts who ravage the garden of the world. Arthur and Artegall do not pause on their way into Mercilla's splendid realm, where Justice and Mercy, strength and compassion, are united. But as instructive as what we see inside is that brief glimpse outside, of the tongue nailed to the post. There the poet has revealed his unshakeable conviction that the man of words must work for the public good, as well as his profound belief in the potency of the poet's art. But while looking into the heart of his calling, Spenser also faces the sources of disorder and chaos. The figure of the mute, banished poet should not simply be read as Moral Spenser punishing a disobedient knave. There is much more faith and much more fear than that concentrated in Malfont. He is finally meant to remind us, monarchs and mere men, that whoever would properly govern, either himself or a nation, must first establish control over the dark and turbulent empire of words.

❧ XI ❧

POETS AND PROTEUS

If one thinks of poets as magicians, as suggested above, then in magicians one can discern types of the poet. And indeed, in the two great wizards of the poem one can see Spenser probing certain dimensions of his ambiguous craft. Archimago is clearly a type of the poet in his sinister aspect. First appearing as an "olde man of pleasing wordes" (I,i,35), he then seeks out "mighty charmes" amidst "magicke bookes, and artes of sundrie kindes" (36).

> Then choosing out few words most horrible,
> (Let none them read) thereof did verses frame. (37)

Spenser, maker of verses, warns us against the words of Archimago, thus inviting the reader to abstain from the very activity the reader at that instant is engaged in. In this way, early on, the reader is introduced to his own version of the dilemma facing the poet: how to participate in the process and products of artistic creation without being implicated in the perils they contain.

Archimago's poetic materials, culled from Hell by blasphemy, are sprights, and of these he chooses two, "fittest for to forge true-seeming lyes" (38). To forge true-seeming lies is, from one perspective, precisely the poet's task, and in the ensuing stanzas Spenser offers us an instance of the process of poetic creation: the choice of a form, the voyage into the subconscious (Morpheus' realm) for a vision, the careful craftsmanship needed to shape the final artifact. And like a poet, Archimago enters sympathetically into his own work of art:

> The maker selfe, for all his wondrous witt,
> Was nigh beguiled with so goodly sight (45)

and, again like the poet, Archimago transfers to his creation something of his own essential nature:

> And that new creature, borne without her dew,
> Full of the makers guyle, with usage sly
> He taught to imitate that lady trew. (46)

"Maker." Spenser does not scruple to apply to the *magus* the hallowed word for poet. As with Error, her books and inky progeny, we do not fully appreciate the significance of Archimago's activities until we have travelled deep into the poem. But, as in life, the farther we go, the more we see how our perceptions were shaped by our beginnings, and the oblique insights into language and its uses found in the opening canto assume ever-expanding richness the more we read.

We begin to understand Archimago better when we come to Merlin in Book III, canto ii. Merlin too is an "arch-magician," "The great magitien" (III,ii,18) who made the mirror in which Britomart saw the image of Artegall, the mirror which

> round and hollow shaped was,
> Like to the world it selfe, and seemd a world of glas.
>
> (III,ii,19)

Here is no creator of false images, but of true reflections—from another perspective, the poet *par excellence*. Unlike Archimago's creations that bring a divisive message, finally separating faith from force (I,i,19), Merlin's artifact gives an integrated vision of all of life. The mirror could

> shew in perfect sight
> What ever thing was in the world contaynd,
> Betwixt the lowest earth and hevens hight,
> So that it to the looker appertaynd.
>
> (III,ii,19)

The glass is like the poem, and Merlin like the poet, or at least the ultimately benign kind of poet checking dark forces, that Spenser wants to be:

> For he by wordes could call out of the sky
> Both sunne and moone, and make them him obay:
> The land to sea, and sea to maineland dry,
> And darksome night he eke could turne to day:
> Huge hostes of men he could alone dismay,

And hostes of men of meanest thinges could frame,
When so him list his enimies to fray:
That to this day, for terror of his fame,
The feends do quake, when any him to them does name.

(III,iii,12)

Whereas Archimago dared call on "Great Gorgon, prince of darknes and dead night" (I,i,37), Merlin advises submission to God and tells Britomart to "submit thy wayes unto His will" (III,iii,24). And unlike Archimago, who appears to Redcross and Una as a result of pursuing Error into her den and who perpetuates error throughout the poem, Merlin expounds the true history of the race Britomart and Artegall will found, a "famous progenee" (III,iii,22) of emperors, kings, and captains who will sustain Britain "Till universall peace compound all civill jarre" (III,iii,23).

Yet for all these differences, and others, for all that guile and dissolution are shadowed in Archimago and the capacity to envision truth and wholeness are figured in Merlin, the two magicians share radical similarities. Both are inhabitants of the periphery, in touch with the darkest powers of earth and man; both are able, through their control of language, to project and shape the destinies of others. Both are makers of worlds beyond the powers of other men but worlds upon which all of us, in essential ways, depend. To the extent to which *The Faerie Queene* is an account of the way our lives are compounded of impulses to self-deception on the one hand and drives to revelation on the other, the poem is an account of the struggle, within each of us, between Archimago and Merlin, between perspective distorted and vision undeflected. But lest we posit too simple a dualism, we must remember that *voyeur* and *voyant,* black and white magician, are finally at one within us all, and that at bottom Spenser is exploring the most deeply rooted impulse of all, man's capacity to create with the mind. Underneath language, Spenser's preoccupation is with the sheer, mute energy from and by which we project new forms, new worlds in the mind to sustain us in the world. In the figures of Archimago and Merlin, the poet surveys that power he has, that process he is engaged in.

Thus far, we have alternated between an Orpheus and a Sclaunder, an Archimago and a Merlin, in tracking the course of the power to make images and that power's fundamental medium of expression, language. But there is one figure in the poem who combines all in himself—not simply the final figure of the poet but also the most pervasive presence in the poem. This figure embodies the dialectic of restraint and dissolution, making and destroying, that is not only at the heart of the poem but is the heart of the poem. This other old man from the deep touches Spenser's every fear and hope. He is the great shape-changer, Proteus, venerable prophet and shepherd of Neptune's flocks.[1]

Book III is the only book of the poem in which Arthur does not appear to initiate a redemptive movement in either canto vii or canto viii. Instead, as I have suggested on page 69, in III,viii, we meet the embodiments of falsity and chaos, the False Florimell and Proteus. Thus, near the center of the poem as we have it, we find the forces of disorder where we have been accustomed to the principle of reassuring strength. This displacement of Arthur, surely no accident, is only one way Spenser underscores the centrality of these forces of dispersal and decay. And Proteus is the focus for them.

To understand Proteus' role in III,viii, we must glance back at his first appearance in III,iv. There, Cymoent, nymph-mother of Marinell, petitioned Proteus in order to learn her son's fate. Proteus

> Bad her from womankind to keepe him well:
> For of a woman he should have much ill;
> A virgin straunge and stout him should dismay or kill.
>
> (III,iv,25)

The hysterically fearful Cymoent teaches Marinell to hate woman's love and so protects her son that he becomes, in one of Spenser's finest similes, "Like as the sacred oxe, that carelesse stands . . ." (III,iv,17)—a hulking, pampered, spoiled boy easily dispatched by Britomart. "So weening to have arm'd him, she did quite disarme" (III,vii,27). This emasculation leads to precisely what it sought to avoid, and at III,vii,28, Spenser muses on life's "double sences," in that passage we have referred to as the center of the poem's meaning. It is proper that this sense of man's ambiguous, "ticklish" state should be so closely associated with Proteus and deep sexual fears, for both the old prophet and those fears are expanded in III,viii.

At III,viii,20, we meet the lovely, hapless Florimell, last seen flee-

ing the vicious hyena who fed on women's flesh (III,vii,26f.). Having
escaped the beast in a fisherman's boat, she is now prey to the
lascivious assaults of the fisherman. At III,viii,29, that old man is
restrained by Proteus, who then takes the terrified girl to his underwater "bowre" (36). Florimell's flight from the hyena to the fisherman to Proteus represents an ascent up the scale of being from beast
to god, but a descent into the depths—symbolized by that bower—
of her worst fears. Florimell, no less than Marinell, is the prisoner
of her fear of the physical and sexual. And after she is kissed and
caressed by Proteus (the frost and icicles from his lips image the
blight this flower fears—III,viii,35), she only stiffens in her resistance
to his wooing. In Ben Jonson's *Volpone*, Volpone, a lesser Proteus,
only promised Celia to meet her in various shapes; Spenser's Proteus
delivers on the spot:

> Dayly he tempted her with this or that,
> And never suffred her to be at rest:
> But evermore she him refused flat,
> And all his fained kindnes did detest,
> So firmely she had sealed up her brest.
> Sometimes he boasted that a god he hight;
> But she a mortall creature loved best:
> Then he would make him selfe a mortall wight;
> But then she said she lov'd none but a Faery knight.

> Then like a Faerie knight him selfe he drest;
> For every shape on him he could endew:
> Then like a king he was to her exprest,
> And offred kingdoms unto her in vew,
> To be his leman and his lady trew:
> But when all this he nothing saw prevaile,
> With harder meanes he cast her to subdew,
> And with sharpe threates her often did assayle,
> So thinking for to make her stubborne corage quayle.

> To dreadfull shapes he did him selfe transforme,
> Now like a gyaunt, now like to a feend,
> Then like a centaure, then like to a storme,
> Raging within the waves: thereby he weend
> Her will to win unto his wished eend.
> But when with feare, nor favour, nor with all
> He els could doe, he saw him selfe esteemd,

Downe in a dongeon deepe he let her fall,
And threatened there to make her his eternall thrall.

(III,viii,39–41)

Proteus' transformations, from god to storm, present the whole scale of being and only confirm Florimell in her fear. But it is important to note that her sexual terror is simply symptomatic of something much deeper. Her basic fear is of letting go, and not being able to reintegrate the self. Her deepest terror is of release without the possibility of restraint. It is a fear imaged throughout the poem in the liquid imagery applied to sex, the figure of drowning, melting, wading, spilling wine (I,i,47; I,vii,7; II,vi,25; III,ix,30–31), all reflecting the fear of the dissolved self. In the cases of Florimell and Marinell (who is translated to his mother's underwater bower), their imprisonment under the sea only reemphasizes that their worst fear is to merge with the natural world in such a way as to lose their distinct shape as a human being. Florimell, who lost her golden girdle at III,vii,31, only to wander at sea and then be assaulted by Proteus, traces for us the terrifying passage from containment and compression—from identity—to dissolution in the undifferentiated natural world—the loss of self.

Proteus is the very essence of formlessness, of deformation as the only formative principle. After all, to be able to take any shape is to have no true shape at all. If you can become anybody, who are you? And finally, shape-changing is not only potentially deceitful and terrifying, it is also potentially blasphemous. For the capacity to imitate all forms is finally only God's power, and to assume it past a certain point is to risk transgressing the proper limits of man. In Proteus, we have an image of the imagination without chains, of the artist as he ceaselessly recreates and challenges the Maker's power.

For all its dangers, however, the Renaissance had also seen this ability to transform the self as man's chief glory. Pico della Mirandola was one of the first in his prefatory *Oration* to *On the Dignity of Man*. There God says to Man:

> Neither a fixed abode nor a form that is thine alone nor any function peculiar to thyself have we given thee, Adam, to the end that according to thy longing and according to thy judgment thou mayest have and possess what abode, what form and what functions thou thyself shalt desire. . . . We have made thee neither of heaven or of earth,

neither mortal nor immortal, so that with freedom of choice and with honor, *as though the maker and molder of thyself, thou mayest fashion thyself in whatever shape thou shalt prefer.* [Italics added]

And then, after exclaiming on the goodness of God, Pico turns to the glory that is man:

Who would not admire this our chameleon? . . . It is man who Aeclepius of Athens, arguing from his mutability of character and from his self-transforming nature, on just grounds says was symbolized by Proteus in the mysteries.²

Yet for poets like Spenser, this faith in and admiration for man's powers of self-transformation was balanced by a deep distrust of sheer, unfettered soaring. Thus, in Spenser's Proteus we have concentrated all the mind's fears about the imagination and the power to transform the self at will. We have the insistent, ancient fear that with no bounds, no chains to wring out the truth, all the carefully fashioned institutions we cherish will be destroyed by man as man looses the power to change his shape, to project new appearances, different realities. If Spenser had not valued the imagination, seat and source of that power, he would not have been so wary of it. The poem finally insists that, in honoring the imagination and all it means, we must not waste this godlike potency, must not deform ourselves where we had hoped to reform the world.

Lest I sound absurdly insistent on Spenser's profoundly mixed feelings about the Protean capacity to project different shapes with the mind, let us see how throughout *The Faerie Queene* the poet returns again and again to the dangers present in the power of transformation. Indeed, in the first figure to embody this power, Archimago, we also have the first warning about losing control:

> He then devisde himselfe how to disguise;
> For by his mighty science he could take
> As many formes and shapes in seeming wise,
> As ever Proteus to himselfe could make:
> Sometime a fowle, sometimes a fish in lake,
> Now like a foxe, now like a dragon fell,
> That of himselfe he ofte for feare would quake,
> And oft would flie away. O who can tell
> The hidden powre of herbes, and might of magicke spel?
>
> (I,ii,10)

Then there was Phantastes, we remember, another old man, like Proteus, who had his chamber decorated with "Infinite shapes of thinges dispersed thin":

> Infernal hags, centaurs, feendes, hippodames,
> Apes, lyons, aegles, owles, fooles, lovers, children, dames.
>
> (II,ix,50)

Not only was Phantastes' chamber the very locus of the imagination, the home of new shapes, but it was also full of buzzing flies, like bees, representing:

> Shewes, visions, sooth-sayes, and prophecies:
> And all that fained is, as leasings, tales and lies.
>
> (II,ix,51)

This seems more an indictment than a description of the imagination; at least it is an account of the dark side of the Protean power.

As we know, the chameleon was a common Renaissance figure for Proteus, and Duessa is endowed with its powers:

> The one of them the false Duessa hight,
> That now had chang'd her former wonted hew:
> For she could d'on so manie shapes in sight,
> As ever could cameleon colours new;
> So could she forge all colours, save the trew.
>
> (IV,i,18)

In ancient myth, Proteus could tell the truth when he was bound; but as the poem progresses, the Protean power loses any capacity to lead to the truth. It only figures the imagination as it counterfeits.

One of the final embodiments of the power of forgery in the latter part of the poem is Malengin, or guile, and he rivals even Proteus himself in new shapes. He appears with accoutrements—a long staff with iron hook and a net on his back (V,ix,11), both of which are intended to catch "fooles," but which also may remind us of the sea and the old sea-shepherd. And like Proteus' are Malengin's abilities, "To leave his proper forme, and other shape to take" (V,ix,16). Pursued by Talus,

> Into a foxe himselfe he first did tourne;
> But he him hunted like a foxe full fast:
> Then to a bush himselfe he did transforme;

> But he the bush did beat, till that at last
> Into a bird it chaung'd, and from him past,
> Flying from tree to tree, from wand to wand:
> But he then stones at it so long did cast,
> That like a stone it fell upon the land;
> But he then took it up, and held fast in his hand.
>
> (V,ix,17)

Upon being brought to Artegall, the stone becomes a hedgehog, and then, hedgehog flung away, tries to become a snake. But Talus relentlessly crushes it with his flail: "So did deceipt the selfe deceiver fayle" (V,ix,19). Once again we learn that deception, pursued far enough, inevitably leads to self-deception. We also witness again the way evil in this poem is the only final check to evil; one must pursue it, out of whatever legal or moral sense we have, but finally we must wait it out. The final form of guile, the snake, reaffirms the fundamentally Satanic nature of the Protean power abused. The snake obliquely emphasizes again that to assume powers of transformation beyond a certain point is to pass the godlike limits of man and challenge the powers of God. It is fitting that the last great Protean figure in European epic will be that ultimate shape-changer, Milton's Satan.

In Book VI, another Protean figure appears. He comes as the savage brigands, abductors of Pastorella, hack each other to pieces underground:

> Thus as they words amongst them multiply,
> They fall to strokes, the frute of too much talke,
> And the mad steele about doth fiercely fly,
> Nor fearing wight, ne leaving any balke,
> But making way for Death at large to walke:
> Who, in the horror of the griesly night,
> In thousand dreadful shapes doth mongst them stalke,
> And makes huge havocke, whiles the candlelight
> Out quenched leaves no skill nor difference of wight.
>
> (VI,xi,16)

This is the fundamental terror in the poem: to be without light, without distinction as a human being. The stanza traces the course we have charted in the last two chapters, from language abused to humanity lost. This is what haunts Spenser, the spectre—beyond words misapplied, beyond deception and guile—of the final and irreversible dissolution. In the power to transform, he sees implicit the power to deform past recognition. He knows the imagination, pure wellhead of glistening and shapely life, is also the dark spring of death. And he fears because he cannot tap that source without releasing both.

The Protean figure of death is made cosmic by Spenser in the final Protean figure, and the great enemy, in the poem, Mutability. This titaness is the very embodiment of all his fears, and her sway on earth is described in precisely the terms we have been examining. She has put a new shape on things:

> For she the face of earthly things so changed,
> That all which Nature had establisht first
> In good estate, and in meet order ranged,
> She did pervert, and all their statutes burst.
>
> (VII,vi,5)

And in the process, she has brought death to all on earth:

> Ne shee the lawes of Nature onely brake,
> But eke of Justice, and of Policie;
> And wrong of right, and bad of good did make,
> And death for life exchanged foolishlie:
> Since which, all living wights have learn'd to die,
> And all this world is woxen daily worse.
> O pittious worke of Mutabilitie!
> By which we all are subject to that curse,
> And death, in stead of life, have sucked from our nurse.
>
> (VII,vi,6)

Change, the Protean essence, is inescapable here, and throughout the *Mutabilitie Cantos* Spenser is careful to admit her hegemony over the sub-lunar world. He is also at pains to distinguish earth from the celestial realm and to make it clear that her sway does not by right extend beyond the earth. Yet "in her ambitious thought," she seeks wider rule and "Jove himselfe to shoulder from his right" (VII,vi,7). And so she plucks Cynthia from her throne on the moon, and the stars are amazed at "her uncouth habit and sterne looke" (VII,vi,13). Yet when Hermes comes to investigate, he is struck by her "straunge sight and haughty hardinesse" (VII,vi,17). A change is taking place. And when she ascends to Jove's palace to argue her case before the gods, they

> marked well her grace,
> Beeing of stature tall as any there
> Of all the gods, and beautiful of face
> As any of the goddesses in place.
>
> (VII,vi,28; see also 31)

As she represents change, so she also changes. Mutability is Proteus writ large, and she threatens to deform and dissolve the whole universe. Yet she is saved from the fate of some of her Protean predecessors when Nature rules against her claim to Heaven by saying simply: ". . . thy decay thou seekst by thy desire" (VII,vii,59). Nature says in effect that if you rule all, you will make yourself permanent and thus cease to be change. So the deceiver is saved from her deceit. She is saved from the consequences of what she embodies. Here, in the seventh canto of Book VII, Nature enacts the role of Arthur; here Nature is the redeemer, turning back Mutability's claim, saving the Heavens for eternity and, in confining corrosive change to earth, providing man with a hope beyond his mortal prison.

The displacement of Arthur by Proteus in Book III is redressed by the greater power of Nature in Book VII. In *The Faerie Queene*, Nature is always the redeemer at last. Through her excellence, we shall be saved—if only we attend her and obey the best in us. As Merlin says to Britomart concerning the family tree she will begin:

> For so must all things excellent begin,
> And eke enrooted deepe must be that tree,
> Whose big embodied braunches shall not lin,
> Til they to hevens hight forth stretched bee.
>
> (III,iii,22)

And yet, to leave the account of Spenser's Proteus here would be to misrepresent badly the Protean impulse in the poem, and indeed badly misrepresent the poem itself. For, as I have said often, the power to transform is also noble and beneficent. Only when completely unfettered does it lead to shapeless evil and horrible dissolution. But if the shaping power is itself shaped, if that energy is restrained for the good, then man fulfills his godlike potential, both as an artist and as a human being. Spenser offers us two superb versions of the restraint of change, where order and energy are wed in a perfect whole. In the first, the marriage of Venus and Adonis, the capacity to change shapes gives, rather than denies, life. After the explanation of the generation of life in the garden of Venus and Adonis in III,vi, we are shown the couple in their arbor on the mount. In that paradise, Venus, the "great mother" (III,vi,40), the principle of matter, loves Adonis.

> And sooth, it seemes, they say: for he may not
> For ever dye, and ever buried bee
> In balefull night, where all thinges are forgot;
> All be he subject to mortalitie,
> Yet is eterne in mutabilitie,
> And by succession made perpetuall,
> Transformed oft, and chaunged diverslie:
> For him the father of all formes they call:
> Therfore needs mote he live, that living gives to all.
>
> (III,vi,47)

Here "transformation" means something quite different from what it will mean in Proteus' cave (and power) two cantos later. Here darkness and death are denied and fecund sexuality affirmed as each new form provides matter with a new shape. If Adonis is a Proteus, and he is, he shows us how transformation can be used to perpetuate life, and he demonstrates how mutability can be fashioned into an image of eternity. Dame Nature will later explain what in Book III Adonis has embodied: that things

> by their change their being doe dilate:
> And turning to themselves at length againe,
> Doe worke their owne perfection so by fate:
> Then over them Change doth not rule and raigne;
> But they raigne over Change, and doe their states maintaine.
>
> (VII,vii,58)

Nature asserts what here Adonis shows, that in divinely ordained change there is permanence; that a providential order informs our daily existence, an existence that only seems to rot itself with motion. In this paradox, in this garden, Spenser weds time and eternity, new shape and old substance, through the union of Adonis and

Venus. III,vi, is a parable of how each of us participates in that
eternal renewal of life which God ordained and is Spenser's concrete, otherworldly version of the paradise within; of what each of
us, through time and generation, can attain.

This whole line of inquiry began with the figure of Proteus in
Book III, and it is to his realm that we return. We saw that the old
shepherd-prophet was a figure of the poet, and that his power to
project new shapes was a way of talking about the imagination.
Then we explored the dark side, so to speak, of the figure and his
power, particularly as they related to language. But Adonis (antici-
pating Dame Nature) has shown us a different side of the power to
transform the self in the garden of Venus and Adonis, and now we
turn to end with Spenser's other great vision of generation and the
imagination. That occurs in Book IV, canto xi, after the vision of
concord and love in the Temple of Venus (IV,x) and after Marinell's
wound is healed and the road to his union with Florimell is pre-
pared (IV,xi,5–7). That vision is the account of the marriage of the
Thames and the Medway.

Though descriptions of the unions of rivers occur earlier in literature, never before had a poet attempted a description of this kind
on such a scale. For fifty-three stanzas he names "all the sea-gods and
their fruitfull seede" (IV,xi,8), the most and the least of the gods

> Aswell which in the mightie ocean trade,
> As that in rivers swim, or brookes doe wade.
>
> (IV,xi,9)

It is a celebration of England through her waters, at the very least
an extraordinary technical accomplishment. But it is, of course,
much more than that. It is finally a venture of the imagination into
the imagination, a gathering together into one place of all those
imaginative springs to form a master image of his own wellhead of
creation. Indeed, the locus of the wedding is precisely that place we
have considered the source of the imagination, for the bride and
groom agree

> that this their bridale feast
> Should for the gods in Proteus house be made.
>
> (IV,xi,9)

Here water is not the shifting, formless element in whose deep we lose our human shape; now water is seen as the stuff of life, the fertile element, imaginatively controlled by figuring it under each sea-god's name, and under the name of each river. Here the name shapes the element, as the element fills out—as it were—the name, and the poet provides us with a splendid pageant about the union of the form that is language with the matter that is meaning, both figured in the names for the stuff of life. In short, Spenser gives us an image of the poetic imagination at work.

In this pageant of concord, the great gods of the sea come first (stanzas 11–19), followed by the famous rivers of the world (20–22), then the poet Arion (23), who precedes the Thames and the English rivers (24–39). Thames wears a "coronet /. . . in which were many towres and castels set" (27), a crown such as Cybele wore in antiquity and which represents the City, in this case Troynovant.[3] Because of Arion's song, once "all the raging seas for joy forgot to rore" (23) and the power of art to curb the forces of nature finds in Thames' turreted crown its ultimate expression. In the midst of the procession, the poet inserts himself and allies his power with civic order and control.

From stanzas 40 to 44, the lovely Irish rivers that Spenser knew so well, each with its own appropriate epithet, pass before us, and then the bride Medway and her English handmaidens (45–47). She is

> Clad in vesture of unknowen geare,
> And uncouth fashion, yet her well became;
> That seem'd like silver, sprinckled here and theare
> With glittering spangs, that did like starres appeare,
> And wav'd upon, like water chamelot,
> To hide the metall, which yet every where
> Bewrayd it selfe, to let men plainely wot,
> It was no mortall worke, that seem'd and yet was not. (45)

The bride's "natural" look sets the tone for her description. Her attire, with its "spangs" (spangles) like stars, that "wav'd" to hide the metal, is a piece of artifice whose art is to look natural. The last six lines of the stanza, comprising one undulating sentence, cunningly merge images to provide an instance of what they describe.

In her flowing hair, Medway wears "flowres bescattered,"

> and likewise on her hed
> A chapelet of sundry flowers she wore. (46)

Flowers and sea, land and water, combine in an artful decoration, culminating in a natural crown corresponding to the groom's imposing civic diadem. The pageant then ends (48–53) with the many daughters of Nereus, the sea-nymphs.

In the marriage procession, Spenser has united male and female, land and water, art and nature, city and garden—all the elements of the world and mind in which and by which we live. He has finally married his powers of invention to the natural world, giving a pageant of concord about the attainment of harmony. The waters present enormous fecundity:

> So fertile be the flouds in generation,
> So huge their numbers, and so numberlesse their nation.
> (IV,xii,1)

Yet he has managed brilliantly to accomplish what he doubted he could do:

> How can they, all in this so narrow verse
> Contayned be, and in small compasse hild?
> (IV,xi,17)

The narrow verse, the furrow of his line, is bursting with the matter he has shaped and controlled, and in this the marriage of the Thames and Medway is another concrete version of the myth of Venus and Adonis. For here the many waters are like Venus, material of the world, and the poet himself is like Adonis, the father of all forms, the shaper. The difference is that in III,vi, the drama of union was recounted through the adaptation of ancient myth; in IV,xi–xii, the drama is enacted as the poet marries the stuff of creation before our eyes, as he, through our eyes, weds his mind to life's matter, thus creating a new myth for the oldest of desires.

Only one figure is missing. Where is Proteus? The spousal takes place in his house, but he appears nowhere. He does not process with the gods, yet Neptune, Glaucus, Phorcys, and all the rest are here. He does not play the host or the guest. In the bower of the imagination, the god is missing. Yet I would assert that he is here;

Proteus is here in the figure or, better, in the presence of Spenser. Spenser has displaced the god (who had displaced Arthur) as the poet has fully assumed his "godlike" power of making, and Proteus has yielded to the ability he signified. Spenser has bound Proteus and the truth has emerged, the glorious pageant that shows in public terms the proper uses to which a man can put those private powers to generate and control new forms.

With the garden of Venus and Adonis, and the marriage of the Thames and Medway, we finish our view of Faery Land. In these two otherworldly visions of our world, the poet has triumphed, at least for the moment, over the problems of transforming energy into order, change into vital permanence. These solutions are meant for the reader. The protagonists of the poem still wander the world, each looking for that visionary answer to his life. But in these two instances, the reader has penetrated to the core, to the clearing at the heart of the poem, and has become a *voyant*, looking directly into the mix and mingle of contending forces out of whose strife harmony emerges. In III,vi, and IV,xi–xii, the greatest marriage poet in English literature asserts that in married sexuality all duality will cease and wholeness, that human kind of holiness, will be ours. In these marriages, the terror of dissolution is overcome by the poet's deepest expectations for life. The imagination he fears is, finally, the source for hope.

Spenser believes in man and in his power to order life, individual and civic, for the better. He finally believes that each of us can achieve that "maystring discipline" necessary to maintain our "faithfull friendship" (IV,ix,2) with each other. What he finally affirms is that humanity compounded of opposed impulses that he loves so much, that humanity he loves, I suspect, as much for, as despite, its frailties.

✑ NOTES ✑

Chapter I

1 I have relied throughout on A. C. Judson's *The Life of Edmund Spenser* (Johns Hopkins University Press, 1945), Vol. VIII of the *Variorum* Spenser; also F. I. Carpenter, *A Reference Guide of Edmund Spenser* (University of Chicago Press, 1923; reprint, Peter Smith, 1950). On the connection with the Spencers, see *Colin Clouts Come Home Againe* (1595), ll. 536–40, and on the three Spencer sisters, Elizabeth, Anne, and Alice, the dedications to *Mother Hubbards Tale, Muipotmos,* and *Teares of the Muses* in *Complaints* (1591).

2 The full title of van der Noot's treatise, first published in Flemish and French, in 1568, is *A Theatre, wherein be represented as wel the miseries and calamaties that follow the voluptuous worldlings as also the greate joyes and pleasures which the faithful do enjoy.* See Judson, *Life,* p. 20.

3 See Judson (*Life,* p. 43 and references) and Carpenter (*Guide,* pp. 125–26), who lists twenty-two titles of "lost" works.

4 I cite the statutes from H. R. Wilson, *The History of Merchant Taylors' School* (London, 1814), pp. 6–17; they are reprinted in F. W. Draper, *Four Centuries of Merchant Taylors' School* (Oxford, 1962), Appendix I.

5 See A. L. Rowse, *The England of Elizabeth* (New York, 1950), p. 491, in the excellent chapter "Education and the Social Order."

6 I cite, by page number in the text, *Positions,* ed. R. A. Quick (London and New York, 1888) and the *Elementarie,* ed. E. T. Campagnac (Oxford, 1925). Both contain good discussions of Mulcaster and his theories, as does J. Oliphant in his collection *The Educational Writings of Richard Mulcaster* (Glasgow, 1903).

7 Judson, *Life,* p. 30. I am indebted in this section on Cambridge to Judson's excellent account of University life.

8 J. C. T. Oates and H. L. Pink, "Three Sixteenth-Century Catalogues of the University Library," *Transactions of the Cambridge Bibliographical Society,* I (1949–1953), pp. 310–40.

9 In 1580, two collections were published at London: *Three proper and wittie familiar Letters* . . . and *Two other very commendable Letters.* . . . These, as well as Harvey's private "letter-book," can be consulted in *The Works of Gabriel Harvey,* ed. A. B. Grosart, 3 volumes (1884–1885, privately printed), Vol. I, which I cite by page number in the text. See also *Gabriel Harvey's Marginalia,* ed. G. C. Moore Smith (Shakespeare Head Press, 1913).

10 I have anticipated in this account, drawing also on Harvey's *Marginalia,* and on Spenser's *Ruines of Time (RT), Ruines of Rome (RR), Teares of the Muses (TM)*—all in *Complaints* (pub. 1591), as well as the *Dedicatory Sonnets* and the *Letter to Ralegh (LR),* to *The Faerie Queene* (1590) and *Colin Clouts Come Home Againe (CCCHA)* and the *Amoretti* (both 1595). All references are to the apparatus of the *Calender* unless otherwise noted.

11 *Marginalia,* ed. Moore Smith, p. 161; see also the envoy to *RR;* for DuBartas, see below, p. 30.

12 For most of the Italian writers and for Mantuan, see below, pp. 29–32.

13 For the *Traveiler,* see *Marginalia,* ed. Moore Smith, p. 173; on the *Howleglass, Marginalia,* p. 23; on all these books, Judson, *Life,* p. 53.

14 In the only prose work of Spenser's that we have, he sets forth his, often savage, remedies for Ireland: *A View of the Present State of Ireland,* published posthumously, Dublin, 1633.

15 See Judson, *Life,* pp. 153–54.

16 Judson, *Life,* p. 198.

17 Jonson and Camden in *Spenser: The Critical Heritage,* ed. R. M. Cummings (London, 1971), pp. 136, 316.

Chapter II

1 *The Poet and His Faith* (University of Chicago Press, 1965), p. 21.

Chapter III

1 Text in *The Pastime of Pleasure,* ed. W. E. Mead, EETS 173 (London, 1928).

Chapter IV

1 This translation by "I.T." has been edited by W. Anderson, Centaur Classics (University of Southern Illinois Press, 1963).

2 In his *Induction,* Sackville says Troy teaches us

> That cities, towres, wealth, world, and all shall quayl
> No manhoode, might, nor nothing mought prevayle.
> (ll. 445–46).

Text in *The Mirror for Magistrates,* ed. Lily B. Campbell (Cambridge University Press, 1938).

3 The two cantos of mutability ("Under the legend of Constancee") VII, vi and vii and two stanzas of viii, were first published in the folio of 1609, ten years after Spenser's death.

4 Text in *The Prologues and Epilogues of William Caxton,* ed. W. J. B. Crotch, EETS 176 (London, 1928), pp. 37, 91.

5 Text in *The Works of Geoffrey Chaucer,* ed. F. N. Robinson, 2nd ed. (Boston, 1957).

Chapter VI

1 In what follows, I am indebted to the introduction of W. E. Mead to *The Famous Historie of Chinon of England* [1597] and Richard Robinson's translation of John Leland's *The Assertion of King Arthur*, EETS 165 (London, 1925); C. B. Millican, *Spenser and the Round Table* (Cambridge, Mass., 1932) and H. Baker, *The Race of Time* (Toronto, 1967).

2 Milton's Monk of Malmsbury, William of Malmsbury (d. 1143?), wrote *De Gestis Regum Angliae* in which Arthur is mentioned as Gawain's uncle. Not a major source.

3 These chronicles did not disappear with the Middle Ages. *The Polychronicon*, Englished in 1387 by John de Trevisa, was printed by Caxton in 1482 and twice again by others by 1527; Hardyng's *Chronicle*, composed ca. 1436, was twice printed by Richard Grafton in 1543. Their popularity is only another instance of how medieval the English Renaissance, like Spenser, would be.

4 Even Caxton, in his prologue to Malory's *Morte Darthur* (1485) had heard "that dyuers men holde oppynyon / that there was no suche Arthur / and that alle suche bookes as been maad of hym / ben but fayned and fables." (*Caxton*, ed. Crotch, p. 93)

5 Cited by Millican, *Spenser and the Round Table*, p. 39.

6 Elizabeth Tudor's Trojan descent continued to be celebrated as well, as at Elvetham in 1591, when Thomas Watson praises her as "beauteous Queene of second Troy"—with none of the melancholy Spenser would associate with Troynovant. (Millican, *Spenser and the Round Table*, p. 37)

7 Texts of following critics drawn from *Elizabethan Critical Essays*, ed. G. G. Smith, 2 vols. (London, 1904).

8 Millican, *Spenser and the Round Table*, p. 53.

Chapter VIII

1 On Pageantry, see Sidney Anglo, *Spectacle, Pageantry and Early Tudor Policy* (Oxford, 1969); David Bergeron, *English Civic Pageantry, 1558-1642* (London, 1971); for a fine overview of where this impulse went, in the drama, see E. Waith, "Spectacles of State," *Studies in English Literature* XIII, 2 (1973), pp. 317-30. Neither Anglo nor Bergeron is concerned to know precisely what the word "pageant" meant.

2 For both occasions, Richard Mulcaster wrote verses (Bergeron, *Pageantry*, p. 31, n. 17).

3 Bergeron, *Pageantry*, p. 30, no. 15, notes the opinion that Laneham's name was probably really John. See his discussion of the Kenilworth entertainment, pp. 30-35.

Chapter IX

1 On this topic, see A. B. Giamatti, "Spenser: From Magic to Miracle" in *Four Essays on Romance*, ed. H. Baker (Harvard University Press, 1971), pp. 17-31.

Chapter X

[1] See Baxter Hathaway, *Marvels and Commonplaces* (New York, 1968), p. 44.

Chapter XI

[1] Proteus was the old sea-god who would change shape until bound—whereupon he would accurately foretell the future. For the role of Proteus and related figures in classical and Renaissance literature, see A. B. Giamatti, "Proteus Unbound: Some Versions of the Sea God in the Renaissance," in *The Disciplines of Criticism*, ed. P. Demetz, T. Greene, L. Nelson (Yale University Press, 1968), pp. 437–75.

[2] Pico della Mirandola, *On the Dignity of Man*, trans. E. L. Forbes in *The Renaissance Philosophy of Man*, ed. E. Cassirer, P. O. Kristeller, and J. H. Randall, Jr. (University of Chicago Press, 1948; Phoenix edition, 1956), pp. 224, 225; on Pico, Proteus, and the chameleon, see Giamatti, "Proteus Unbound," pp. 439f.

[3] For Cybele's crown, see Lucretius, *De Rerum Natura* II, 609f.; Virgil, *Aeneid* VI, 784–85; Ovid, *Fasti* IV, 249.

◆§ BIBLIOGRAPHY §◆

BIBLIOGRAPHY

Bayley, Peter, "Spenser," in *English Poetry Select Bibliographical Guides,* ed. A. E. Dyson (Oxford, 1971), pp. 14–39.

STUDIES IN THE EPIC

Green, Thomas, *The Descent from Heaven* (New Haven and London, 1963).

Durling, Robert, *The Figure of the Poet in Renaissance Epic* (Cambridge, Mass., 1965).

Giamatti, A. B., *The Earthly Paradise and the Renaissance Epic* (Princeton, 1966).

Steadman, John M., *Milton and the Renaissance Hero* (Oxford, 1967).

BACKGROUND

Greenlaw, E., C. G. Osgood, F. M. Padelford et al., eds., *The Works of Edmund Spenser, A Variorum Edition,* 9 volumes (Baltimore, 1934–1949; rev. ed., 1958; Index Vol., 1963).

Tuve, Rosamund, *Allegorical Imagery* (Princeton, 1968).

Starnes, D. T., and E. W. Talbert, *Classical Myth and Legend in Renaissance Dictionaries* (Chapel Hill, 1955).

Bush, Douglas, *Mythology and the Renaissance Tradition in English Poetry,* rev. ed. (New York, 1963).

Lotspeich, Henry, *Classical Mythology in the Poetry of Edmund Spenser* (Princeton, 1932; reprint, New York, 1965).

GENERAL STUDIES

Renwick, W. L., *Edmund Spenser* (London, 1925).

Hamilton, A. C., *The Structure of Allegory in 'The Faerie Queene'* (Oxford, 1961).

Nelson, William, *The Poetry of Edmund Spenser* (New York and London, 1963).

Lewis, C. S., *The Allegory of Love* (Oxford, 1936; rev. ed., 1938).

———, *Spenser's Images of Life,* ed. A. D. S. Fowler (Cambridge, 1967).

Fowler, A. D. S., *Spenser and the Numbers of Time* (London, 1964).

Cheney, Donald, *Spenser's Image of Nature* (New Haven, 1966).

Williams, Kathleen, *Spenser's World of Glass* (Berkeley and Los Angeles, 1966).

Alpers, Paul J., *The Poetry of 'The Faerie Queene'* (Princeton, 1967).

Hankin, John E., *Source and Meaning in Spenser's Allegory* (New York, 1971).

STUDIES OF INDIVIDUAL BOOKS

Book II
Berger, Harry, *The Allegorical Temper* (New Haven, 1957).

Books III and IV
Roche, Thomas P., *The Kindly Flame* (Princeton, 1964).

Book V
Dunsheath, Thomas K., *Spenser's Allegory of Justice in Book V of "The Faerie Queene"* (Princeton, 1968).

Aptekar, Janet, *Icons of Justice: Iconography and Thematic Imagery in Book V of "The Faerie Queene"* (New York, 1969).

Book VI
Williams, Arnold, *Flower on a Lowly Stalk* (East Lansing, 1967).

Tonkin, Humphrey, *Spenser's Courteous Pastoral* (New York, 1972).